Real Cheesy Facts About: TV & Movies

CRANE HILL
PUBLISHERS

Real Cheesy Facts About: TV & Movies

ISBN-13: 978-1-57587-249-0
ISBN-10: 1-57587-249-8

Book design by Miles G. Parsons
Illustrations by Tim Rocks and Miles G. Parsons

Printed in the United States of America

Library of Congress Cataloging-in-Publication Data

Platt, Camille Smith.
  Real cheesy facts about-- television & movies / by Camille
Smith Platt.
     p. cm.
  ISBN-13: 978-1-57587-249-0
  1. Television broadcasting--United States--Miscellanea. 2.
Motion
pictures--United States--Miscellanea. I. Title.

  PN1992.3.U5P53 2006
  791.450973--dc22

2006024773

Real Cheesy Facts About: TV & Movies

Camille Smith Platt

CRANE HILL
PUBLISHERS

TABLE OF CONTENTS

Chapter 1

⭐

Stories from the Set

Stories from the Set

★ ★ ★ ★ ★ ★ ★ ★ ★ ★ ★ ★ ★ ★ ★ ★ ★

Some pretty unusual things happen on the sets of movies and television shows—props get mixed up, and costars posing as lovers in a script can't stand each other in real life. Directors do their best to deal with prima donnas, and fans turn their backs on hosts for the sake of a big settlement. You haven't heard it all until you've heard these wacky tales from some of the most popular sets of all time.

On the classic TV series *I Love Lucy*, the Ricardos supposedly lived at 623 E. 68th Street in Manhattan. However, the real E. 68th Street ends at 600, meaning their building would be located in the East River.

★ ★ ★ ★ ★

LUCY, YOU'VE GOT SOME COMPLAINING TO DO

A veteran hypocrite of feel-good sitcoms, *I Love Lucy* may have been full of canned laughter in the 1950s—but **thanks to actress Vivian Vance, the moods on set weren't as chipper as one might imagine.** Before she was hired as Lucy's quick-witted neighbor, Ethel Mertz, Vance suffered a bout with depression and multiple psychosomatic diseases that led her to quit the popular show *The Voice of the Turtle*.

BEFORE SHE WAS A STAR... VIVIAN VANCE

Born Vivian Roberta Jones in Cherryvale, Kansas, in 1909, she had dreams of being a star from a young age. Her strictly religious parents refused to let her pursue her passion, but at age sixteen she left home to be a stage actress regardless. After a stint of bad luck, she gave up and returned to Kansas—but the early retirement wouldn't last long. In her twenties, she changed her name to Vivian Vance and gave it another shot on Broadway alongside Jimmy Durante and Bob Hope.

Regardless, Desi Arnaz was a fan of her work and offered her the part. However, Lucy wasn't all that excited about her new costar.

Eager to be the only beauty with a major role, Ball had initially envisioned Ethel as a chunky housewife in smelly slippers. Vance was hot stuff—and just a few years older than she. In the end, Ball caved to her husband's vision for the comedy and agreed that Vance would have to do.

TIDBITS OF I LOVE LUCY TRIVIA

- The show was based on Lucille Ball and Richard Denning's popular radio program, *My Favorite Husband*. When it was turned into a sitcom, however, Ball dumped Denning for her real-life husband, Cuban-born Desi Arnaz. Although producers feared American audiences would not buy into a mixed marriage, Ball got her way.

- Ethel's middle name changed multiple times during the show's airing. It switched from Mae to Roberta to Louise.

- The kitchen at the Mertz's apartment was shown in only one episode.

- Lucille Ball liked to name new characters after people from her real life. Marion Strong, for example, was one of her friends from Jamestown, New York, and Carolyn Appleby was one of her old teachers. Ball also named places on the show after favorite locales from her personal life. Lucy and Ricky were married at Byram River Beagle Club in Greenwich, Connecticut—just like Ball and Arnaz.

If the tension between the two leading ladies wasn't enough, actor William Frawley (who played Ethel's husband, Fred Mertz) was just as much a grump offscreen as he was onscreen. He was chronically annoyed by the detailed practice Vance would put into perfecting her character. He also complained about their more than twenty year age difference. To Frawley, the spread was simply too great to pull off being her spouse.

Seems like Lucy may have some 'splaining to do about some things going on at her former home. Though she died during surgery on April 26, 1989, at the age of 77, some people say she's still living at 100 North Roxbury Drive. Current owners say that windows are broken by unseen forces, loud voices are heard from the attic, and furniture and other objects move around.

But Lucy's not the only one of her generation that's having a hard time leaving the spotlight. Here's a few of her fellow actors that have been seen still taking curtain calls:

- **Montgomery Cliff**—He's been seen at the Hollywood Roosevelt Hotel, particularly in room 928, where he paced the floor as he learned his lines for *A Place in the Sun* and *From Here to Eternity*.

- **Marilyn Monroe**—Also a frequent guest at the Hollywood Roosevelt, where she's seen reflected in a full-length mirror that used to be by her pool. She is sometimes seen at the home where she took a fatal dose of sleeping pills, where she reportedly told psychics that her death was an accident, not suicide.

- **Ozzie Nelson**—The spirit of this family patriarch has been seen at the home where he and Harriet lived for forty years. His spirit is not as well mannered as he was on his TV series *The Adventures of Ozzie and Harriet*. He's said to open and close doors, and to turn on faucets and lights.

★ ★ ★ ★ ★

LIGHTS, CAMERA, ABSENT

I Love Lucy wasn't the only set to struggle with tensions between cast members. While taping episodes of *The Honeymooners*, **actor Jackie Gleason refused to rehearse**, explaining that in order for his comedy to be off-the-wall, each performance needed to be fresh. He carried such power on set (he even got the nickname "The Great One") that he got his way, and everyone else had to rehearse their lines without him. The situation put so much stress on costar Audrey Meadows that she often cried out in frustration. Not knowing what to expect when Gleason took the stage, she had no way to fully prepare for each scene.

★ ★ ★ ★ ★

ADDING ALCOHOL TO INJURY

The Bourne Identity star **Matt Damon has come a long way** since his one-line debut in the 1988 film *Mystic Pizza* with fellow Hollywood fledgling Julia Roberts—and no one goes to extremes to prepare for time on the set like he does. On more than one occasion, Damon has submitted himself to injuries and desperate drunks to get his characters just right:

- He damaged most of the major organs in his body when he fasted—without being under a doctor's supervision—to lose nearly forty pounds for his role in *Courage Under Fire*.

- He separated a rib while practicing his golf swing for *The Legend of Bagger Vance*.

- He worked as a bartender in Knoxville, Tennessee, to study up on Southern accents and mixing drinks.

Actor Tom Hanks is another Hollywood superstar willing to go to extremes to prepare for roles. He has...

- Dislocated his shoulder falling through a rotten floor while helping Steven Spielberg pick out a location to tape the HBO show *Band of Brothers* in Germany.

- Gained thirty pounds eating ice cream to prepare for his role in *A League of Their Own* and lost thirty pounds to prepare for his role in *Philadelphia*.

- Got a staph infection in his leg that required emergency surgery while filming overseas.

- However daring Hanks may be, however, there is one thing he refused to do—he would not learn how to write with his left hand to accurately portray his character in *Apollo 13*.

★ ★ ★ ★ ★

I CRY WITH MY LITTLE EYE

Jay Leno has long been a leading funnyman of late night comedy. However, during one taping in 1998, unsuspecting *Tonight Show* audience member Stewart Gregory of Cincinnati, Ohio, was smacked in the face by a free

T-shirt the crew had fired into the crowd with an air gun. Instead of praising his prize like most guests, Gregory brought a lawsuit against Leno and NBC, claiming he had been "battered" and "forcefully struck." Just what did he need to get over the little incident? More than $25,000 in damages to cover his emotional distress, humiliation, and unending pain and suffering.

★ ★ ★ ★ ★

Like Pulling Teeth, Literally

While preparing to hit the set to tape the 1984 war flick *Birdy*, **Nicolas Cage decided that the only way to research the true emotional condition of a maimed war veteran was to submit himself to something terribly painful.** In order to fully understand his character, he had several teeth pulled without novocaine. He later sacrificed his pucker (and his pride) for the sake of character development. In the late 1980s, he turned down a plastic prop bug and actually agreed to eat a live cockroach for *Vampire's Kiss*.

A Koosh to the Pucker

Rosie O'Donnell suffered a nasty $3 million lawsuit when a seventy-one-year-old widow complained of being hit in the mouth with a Koosh ball while attending a taping of Rosie's show in 2001. Not only did it cause her gums to bleed and swell, she contested, but the pain made her spend Christmas alone at home and put a damper on her relationship with her boyfriend.

★ ★ ★ ★ ★

Cox's Identity Crisis

They say first impressions are everything, but actress Courteney Cox would probably disagree. Few people know that she was originally scripted to play twenty-something daddy's girl Rachel Green on the sitcom *Friends*, but she changed her mind and chose the part of the obsessive-compulsive Monica Geller

TIDBITS OF FRIENDS TRIVIA

- The show was originally titled *The Six of Us*.

- Phoebe's porn star twin sister, Ursula, first appeared in a reoccurring role on the NBC sister sitcom *Mad About You*. Producers worried that viewers might be confused when they realized actress Lisa Kudrow was playing in two similar sitcoms at once, so they wrote Ursula into the Friends script to make light of the situation. They got even wittier when they had Helen Hunt make a cameo in a *Friends* episode mistaking Phoebe for Ursula.

- Gunther from Central Perk Coffee Shop, played by struggling actor James Michael Tyler, was just an extra during the first season of the show. He only had one line all year, but when producers realized he was the only extra who could actually work an espresso machine (in real life he had a part time job at a coffee shop), they made his part permanent.

instead. Cox says she just couldn't turn down Monica's sarcasm and strength. She told producers she related to Geller more, and the part was hers. As she settled into the new role in the early 1990s, Cox said that she and her cast mates had no clue how popular their sitcom was until they traveled to London to shoot the episode in which Ross and Emily get married. Paparazzi were everywhere, and they suddenly realized they were big stars.

★ ★ ★ ★ ★

I've Got A Golden Dance Number

When brainstorming choreography for the 1971 hit musical Willy Wonka and the Chocolate Factory starring Gene Wilder, Director Mel Stuart got a little nauseated when it came to coming up with the characters' dance moves for the song "I've Got a Golden Ticket." Because Charlie and Grandpa Joe had just found the fifth and final ticket for a

THE CANDY MAN CAN'T

Quaker Oats originally bought the rights to Charlie and the Chocolate Factory from author Roald Dahl and then agreed to fully finance the making of the film in exchange to use it as a marketing ploy for their new candy bar, the Wonka Bar. However, for various reasons, including a faulty formula, the chocolate bar never made it to the marketplace.

grand tour of the mysterious local candy factory, choreographer Howard Jeffery felt a little pressure to make the number a major production—but Stuart just couldn't imagine the entire town leaving work to sing and dance in the street in celebration of a little boy's candy bar. Instead, he opted for a simple tune… in a dilapidated shack with Charlie's four bedridden grandparents—who, according to the plotline, hadn't gotten up in the last twenty years. Not exactly what Hollywood would call an exciting Oscar-winning moment, but it fit the budget (and Stuart's idea of reality).

It's been rumored that Fred Astaire almost played Willy Wonka in the original *Willy Wonka and the Chocolate Factory*. Director Mel Stuart was looking for someone nutty, screwy and loony, and "someone who could sing." However, Astaire was never in the running for the part. The film's composer, Leslie Bricusse, was indeed a good friend of the famed dancer and apparently had lightheartedly discussed the opportunity with Astaire, but if he was interested, the news never got back to the film's producers or director.

Astaire was seventy-two at the time—too old—and they couldn't have afforded him anyway. They considered Joel Grey, who had recently acted in *Cabaret* on Broadway, but he was only 5'5"… the same height as some of the children.

Gene Wilder, who was finally chosen for the part, wasn't yet a comedic legend, but he was working on it. His persona was slowly gaining fame through his parts in *Bonnie and Clyde* and *The Producers*. Dave Wopler took one look at Wilder's wirey hair and sneaky grin and said, "That's a Willy Wonka."

★ ★ ★ ★ ★

GURU TO THE DUKE

The spitting image of a traditional cowboy, Wyatt Earp was quiet and stern-faced, but approachable. Living in Los Angeles, California, in the early 1900s, he often dropped by Hollywood movie sets to visit friends, and eventually befriended silent western film star William S. Hart. A sucker for butting in on rehearsals, Earp did what he could to teach Hart how to draw his gun with greater speed. By the time he was nearly eighty years old, Earp had such a traditional look of Western wisdom that he impressed prop man Marion Morrison on the set of yet another film. A young gun in the movie business, Morrison was affected by him forever—he changed his name to John Wayne and scored his first starring role in *The Big Trail*. Later, Wayne would tell friends that during his many years as a prop man, he had studied how to act like a true cowboy by simply watching Earp.

★ ★ ★ ★ ★

AN ELEPHANT NEVER REGRETS

When a cooky clown makes a cameo on a classic TV Land sitcom, viewers are usually in for a cheesy sight gag. One sidesplitting episode of **The Mary Tyler**

John Wayne is the record holder for the actor with the most leading parts in films. He starred in 142 movies during his lifetime.

Moore Show features the sad but laughable death of **Chuckles the Clown,** who was crushed by an elephant while parading around in a peanut suit. When Moore first read the script, however, she didn't find the scene very funny. Regardless of her ploy to stop the merciless moment, the rest of the cast and crew got so tickled by the writers' creativity that they just couldn't stop laughing when they saw the trample take place on set. Moore lost her battle to change the scene, and Chuckles' fate was sealed.

★ ★ ★ ★ ★

A Barefoot Beauty

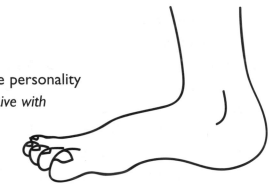

Not one to hide her cute personality and quirky sense of humor, *Live with Regis and Kelly* cohost **Kelly Ripa often hosts entire episodes of her bubbly morning show barefoot.** Viewers must not mind pondering her pedicured toes, because she was named one of *People* magazine's "25 Most Intriguing People" in 2001 and has been nominated for eight Daytime Emmy Awards.

BEFORE SHE WAS A STAR... KELLY RIPA

Kelly Ripa could be seen shaking her rump as a regular on the afternoon teen music program *Dance Party USA* in the late 1980s. Just a few years later, her first television role was as gothic teen Hayley Vaughan on the soap opera *All My Children*.

★ ★ ★ ★ ★

DRIVING MRS. BRADY

On the set of *The Brady Bunch*, during several seasons of taping, **Mike and Carol Brady sported a confusing, inconsistent array of autos**.

DOORS TO NOWHERE

On the set of *The Brady Bunch*, the door at the top of the stairs is never opened.

For the first two seasons, the family boasted a sporty blue 1969 Plymouth Fury convertible and a more practical, less-than-impressive 1969 Plymouth Satellite station wagon. The following year, however, the Plymouth Fury was replaced with a blue 1971 Plymouth Barracuda, and the station wagon was magically updated to a 1971 model.

While Carol's station wagon stuck around for a few more seasons, Mike Brady just couldn't keep a car. He may have been

A VERY BRADY TRESPASSING

Just inside the city limits of Los Angeles, California (11222 Dilling Street, to be exact), lies the split-level home that will forever be flocked with tourists hoping to peek through the blinds to catch a glimpse of any traces of the Bradys left inside. Regardless of remodeling projects done by previous owners to make the house less recognizable, unwelcome trespassers continue to poke around the yard. Unfortunately for the peeping toms, they may catch a glimpse of the current owner, but they will never spy any props from the show. The cast never actually filmed there. The house was used for exterior shots only.

leasing, but the plotline didn't give any hints to viewers who may have been confused by the mysterious upgrades.

The vehicles just kept switching on set without an explanation, which by 1972 were Chevrolets instead of Chryslers.

- 1972-1973—Mike Brady drives a 1972 Chevrolet Impala (blue).

- 1973-1974—Mike Brady drives a 1973 Chevrolet Caprice Classic convertible (maroon with white interior). Halfway through the season, the car is suddenly red with a sleek *black* interior.

- 1988—For the film *A Very Brady Christmas*, both the ever-upgrading Chevrolet and the family station wagon disappear in exchange for a 1988 Chrysler LeBaron.

- 1990—For the short-lived series *The Bradys*, Mike drives the same car as in *A Very Brady Christmas*, but the station wagon (now a 1990 Buick Estate) reappears as the car Marcia swerves about in when she has too much to drink.

★ ★ ★ ★ ★

WHERE EVERYBODY KNOWS YOU'RE LATE

Some say you can tell a man by the clothes he wears, but on the set of *Cheers*, actress **Shelley Long took the tip to the extreme**. She gave her costars a healthy dose of stress every time she headed back to her dressing room to

update her duds. Always labeled as the black sheep among the bar buddies, Long was often blamed for delaying taping because she took so long to change from one outfit to another. Her tardiness got so bad that the crew built her a new dressing room closer to the set, hoping it would keep her from blaming her tardiness on the long walk. In the end, the writers just started keeping her scenes to one twenty-four-hour period so there wouldn't be a need to change clothes mid-taping.

★ ★ ★ ★ ★

PEE PEE RAYMOND REMINISCES

Directors have long discovered that not every laughable thing said on set is fictional. In one episode of the award-winning sitcom *Everybody Loves Raymond*, **Ray reminisces on his childhood nickname "Pee Pee Raymond,"** which credited him with using the bathroom on home base during a Little League baseball game. The tale is actually a true story from Romano's childhood. Carrying the joke over to the scriptwriters, the comedian even changed the

TIDBITS OF EVERYBODY LOVES RAYMOND TRIVIA

- The cereal that always appears on top of Ray and Debra Barone's refrigerator is a box of Flutie Flakes.

- Although Raymond's brother, Robert, is cast as four years older, he is actually three years younger in real life.

- The actress who plays Robert's wife, Amy, is the wife of the show's executive producer.

23

credits at the end of the episode to replace the usual "Ray Romano" with "Pee Pee Raymond."

A long-time comedian, Romano is also known to joke during filming about how jealous he is of fellow funnyman Jerry Seinfeld, who celebrated nine years of filming his own sitcom *Seinfeld* before it went off the air in 1998. Since then, *Everybody Loves Raymond* has celebrated the same success. Besides Seinfeld, however, Romano says comedy legend Bill Cosby is his greatest influence. In fact, Cosby once talked decision-makers at CBS into moving *Everybody Loves Raymond* from airing Friday nights to airing Mondays in order to help boost ratings. His generous suggestion was a hit, and Romano's sitcom became one of the network's most popular shows ever. Before the sitcom aired its final episode in 2005, Romano was reportedly the highest paid television actor in history. In 2001, alone he made $19 million.

BEFORE HE WAS A STAR... RAY ROMANO

Born December 21, 1957, in Queens, New York, Ray Romano had dreams of becoming an accountant before giving up number crunching in exchange for something more laughable—comedy. As his career blossomed, Romano was originally cast as Joe in the short-lived sitcom *NewsRadio*, but was fired when executives decided his dry humor didn't mesh with the rest of the cast.

From his very first standup routine, comedian Ray Romano has been an avid supporter the New York Police Department, where his brother is a sergeant. In 2000, Romano won $125,000 for the NYPD's D.A.R.E. Program on, *Who Wants To Be A Millionaire.*

★ ★ ★ ★ ★

CROSS FOR GUN CONTROL

Rosie O'Donnell was once the queen of daytime television and K-Mart commercials across the globe. Publicly announcing her sexual orientation as a lesbian may have caused her days as a talk show host to hit the skids, but it was her love affair with gun control that took her off the set for good. After writing (and starring in) a handful of commercials for the one-stop shop K-Mart with friend Penny Marshall, O'Donnell called it quits when she realized the chain sold more guns than nearly any other store.

★ ★ ★ ★ ★

PINK SLIP FOR POSING NUDE

After sowing her wild oats posing for a nine-page spread in the December 1993 issue of *Playboy*, **actress Shannen Doherty was sent packing** from the set of the popular sitcom *Beverly Hills, 90210*. Executives were embarrassed, and she was so bitter for losing her job that when The Fox Network aired a

one-hour reunion special years later, she refused to give them permission to show footage of her. To avoid breaking copyright laws,

DID YOU KNOW?

Beverly Hills High School is actually zoned for the area code 90212.

the network had to blur out her face from every flashback. Five years later, Doherty pulled herself together to play the telekinesis big sister witch Prue on the WB sitcom *Charmed*. However, after costar Alyssa Milano began getting more press attention, a jealous Doherty tried to quit the show. Producers wouldn't let her out of the contract, but the animosity between the two stars became so unbearable that Doherty got her wish and got fired anyway. She would later go on to say that she regretted wasting three years of her life on a sitcom "for 12 year olds." Can anyone say "bitter?"

★ ★ ★ ★ ★

HARD LESSONS

Animal House (1978)
The Set: The University of Oregon
   Because of his tight budget for
the film, Universal Pictures director
John Landis decided that instead of building a
set, he would use an actual college campus. After being turned down

by the University of Missouri-Columbia's president when he read the script, the University of Oregon's dean agreed. He had previously been the president of a small California college, and had denied permission to film *The Graduate* at his school. He didn't make that mistake twice. The only off-campus building filmed was an old halfway house for criminals which was used for exterior shots of the Delta house. When it was torn down in 1986, the bricks were sold as souvenirs for $5 each.

> The Motion Picture Production Code, self-imposed guidelines for the industry, were published in 1934, and continued to influence Hollywood until the 1950s.

★ ★ ★ ★ ★

FAMOUS SET LOCALES

The Birds (1963)
The Set: Bodega Bay, California

One of Hitchcock's most classic horror flicks, *The Birds* was filmed just north of San Francisco. The haunting house still stands as a private home today.

The Bridges of Madison County (1995)
The Set: Winterset, Iowa

Located just thirty miles southwest of Des Moines, only six out of the nineteen bridges originally built in the town and shown in the film *The Bridges of Madison County* are still standing today. The farmhouse where Italian housewife Francesca (Meryl Streep) lived became a tourist attraction until a fire in 2003.

The Alamo (1960)
The Set: Mexico and Texas

Made for a jaw dropping $8 million, *The Alamo* was the most expensive movie ever made when it came out in 1960. In fact, filming got so costly that director John Wayne moved the set out of Mexico to a four hundred-acre ranch in Bracketville, Texas (about a hundred miles west of San Antonio). The original set still exists and is used for filming other movies.

Carrie (1976)
The Set: Hermosa Beach Community Center

The official backdrop for the fiery prom scene where high school reject Carrie lost her cool and wreaked havoc on her teasing classmates, the community center in Hermosa Beach, California, was home to one of the most chilling horror flicks of all time. Today, the gym looks nearly the same as it did during filming—minus the spilled bucket of pig's blood that fell from the sky onto the jaded prom queen played by Sissy Spacek.

Fast Times at Ridgemont High (1982)
The Set: Canoga Park High School in Canoga Park, California, and Van Nuys High School in Van Nuys, California

Written by Hollywood mogul Cameron Crowe, *Fast Times at Ridgemont High* used the two high schools for filming, and the set for mall scenes was Sherman Oaks Galleria in Sherman Oaks, California, which has since been renovated into an office complex.

Ghostbusters (1984)

The Set: New York and Los Angeles

While most of the scenes were shot in California, the exterior shots of the Ghostbuster headquarters were of a fire station located at 14 North Moore Street in New York City. The exterior shots of the apartment building where Dana Barrett (Sigourney Weaver) lived were on Central Park West.

DID YOU KNOW

Rumors have long suggested that the Ghostbusters logo was drawn based on the likeness of actor Jim Belushi.

Jurassic Park (1993)

The Set: Hawaiian islands of Oahu and Kauai

This daring dinosaur hit was filmed across the beautiful Garden Isles of Hawaii. The giant gates at the opening of Jurassic Park were off Blue Hole Canyon, and the electrical fence that T-Rex tore through was in Kauai's Olokele Valley. The "Badlands" scene at the beginning of the movie was not filmed in Utah, as implied, but at Red Rock Canyon in California's Mojave Desert.

Rocky (1976)
The Set:

• The gym where the film's opening fight scene takes place—Oscar de la Hoya Boxing Youth Center in Los Angeles, California

• The butchery where Rocky trained for his title fight punching hanging beef—Shamrock Meats, Inc. in Vernon, California

• The museum where Rocky ran to the top of the famous sixty-eight-step staircase pumping his arms in victory—Philadelphia Museum of Modern Art in Philadelphia, Pennsylvania

• Famous fight scenes with Apollo Creed—Olympic Auditorium in Los Angeles and Los Angeles Memorial Sports Arena

★ ★ ★ ★ ★

OTHER FAMOUS SETS

• **National Lampoon's Vacation**—Family vacation to Wally World was filmed at Six Flags Magic Mountain in Valencia, California.

• **Top Gun**—Eatery where Anthony Edwards pounds out "Great Balls of Fire" on the piano is the Kansas City Barbeque Restaurant in San Diego, California.

• **When Harry Met Sally**—The restaurant where Meg Ryan had her fake orgasm was filmed in Katz's Deli in East Village, New York City. Today a plaque in the deli reads, "You are sitting where Harry met Sally."

• **Raiders of the Lost Ark**—While most of the film was shot in Kauai, France, England, and Tunisia, the classroom where Indiana (actor Harrison Ford) teaches archaeology was shot at the Conservatory of Music at the University of the Pacific in Stockton, California.

★ ★ ★ ★ ★

ACCIDENTS AND TRAGEDIES ON THE SET

- **Harrison Ford**—In January of 2003, this veteran actor was riding in a car driven by co-star Josh Hartnett during filming of his movie, *Hollywood Homicide*, when the vehicle went out of control and hit a wall. A source on the set admitted that the scenario should have been done by stuntmen, but "Harrison insists on doing all of his stunts, so his co-star Josh didn't want to be left out." The pair was lucky—they came through the incident with only a bump on the head and some pulled muscles between the two of them.

- **Brandon Lee**—An actor who earned acclaim in his own right, Lee was the son of legendary martial artist and actor Bruce Lee and Linda Emery. Bruce died suddenly from a cerebral edema when Brandon was eight. Young Brandon was often described as "a handful" by his mother, not to mention his teachers. At school, he was "either the teacher's pet, or the teacher's nightmare."

    Expelled from Chadwick School three months before graduating, Brandon followed his father into acting, and was part of the American New Theatre group founded by his friend John Lee Hancock. His first movie was *Legacy of Rage*, which also included Bolo Yeung, who had appeared in his father's last film.

Later, in Los Angeles, he was asked to audition for a role in *Kung Fu: The Movie*, a feature-length television movie. Lee got the role, due to the increasing posthumous fame of his father. He would become an important figure in not one, but two, sequels to the famous TV series.

Other acting assignments followed and Lee signed a multi-picture deal with 20th Century Fox. In 1992, he landed the role of Eric Draven, who returned from death to avenge his and his fiancée's murders, in the movie adaptation of *The Crow*, a popular underground comic book. Shooting began on February 1, 1993, Lee's twentieth birthday. It would be his last.

On March 31, 1993, the fifty-second day of a sixty-day shooting schedule, Lee's scene called for him to confront his fiancée's attacker, and subsequently be shot. Since production was slightly behind schedule, dummy cartridges would be made from real cartridges. The effects technician dismmantled them by removing the bullets, emptying out the gunpowder, detonating the primer, and reinserting the bullets. Some blanks were created by replacing gunpowder with firework powder, and not inserting the bullets. Though Lee was shot with a cartridge without its own bullet, there was a bullet in the gun from a previous shot, which was propelled out by the blank cartridge's explosion. Lee was shot and severely wounded, and the whole thing was caught on film at Carolco Studios in Wilmington, North Carolina. By the time the wound in Lee's abdomen was discovered, he was unconscious. Doctors fought for five hours to save his life, but he was pronounced dead at 1:04 p.m. His funeral was held several days later, and he was buried next to his father in Lake View Cemetery, Capitol Hill, in Seattle, Washington.

- **_Eva Longoria_**—This desperate housewife was rushed to the hospital when a piece of equipment fell on her head during filming of an episode of the hit series. She was taken to a nearby hospital, but released after treatment. Her spokesperson assured everyone, "She's just fine. It was a big jolt but she has a hard head. She's tough!"

- **_Vic Morrow_**—When Morrow died tragically in a helicopter accident during the filming of _Twilight Zone—the Movie_, Hollywood lost a veteran actor whose skills honed over a lifetime of acting would be sorely missed. But if that loss weren't enough, two children—Myca Dinh Le and Renee Shin-Yi Chen—were also killed.

Morrow was not a fan of helicopters anyway. Oddly enough, earlier in his career, when he was filming _Dirty Mary Crazy Larry_, there was a scene where he was supposed to fly in a helicopter. He said, "I'm not getting up in the helicopter. . . I have a premonition that I'm going to get killed in a helicopter crash."

That prophecy came true at 2:20 a.m. on July 23, 1982, as the final shot of a _Twilight_ sequence was being recorded. Morrow was supposed to have the two children in his arms as he waded across a knee-deep river. A village under siege was in the background as the helicopter came to rescue them. Director John Landis ordered the helicopter increasingly lower, until it was finally a mere twenty-four feet above the water.

As explosions were going off all around, the pilot lost control of the helicopter, which came to rest on top of Renee, crushing her. Morrow and the other child, Myca Le, were decapitated by the forty-foot blades.

The announcement was immediately made, "Leave your equipment where it is. Everyone go home. Please, everyone go home!"

Vic Morrow's funeral took place two days later. John Landis gave a eulogy before Morrow's burial at Hillside Memorial Park. Landis also attended funerals held for the children on July 27. Renee is buried in Forest Lawn, Glendale, Myca Le in buried in Cerritos.

On a more positive note, the accident led to massive reforms in U.S. child labor laws and safety regulations on movie sets in California.

Chapter 2

★

Regret: Hollywood's Biggest Bombs

Regret: Hollywood's Biggest Bombs

★ ★ ★ ★ ★ ★ ★ ★ ★ ★ ★ ★ ★ ★ ★

To quote German Chancellor Konrad Adenauer, "In view of the fact that God limited the intelligence of man, it seems unfair that he did not also limit his stupidity." There are easier ways of getting attention than by royally screwing up what should have been an amazing movie. But some directors just didn't get the memo. Love 'em or hate 'em, you just can't help but ask: How could so many good ideas go so wrong?

There were plans for big-name *M*A*S*H* stars like Alan Alda to make special guest appearances in the second season of *AfterMASH*, but the show was canceled before any such plans could be carried out.

★ ★ ★ ★ ★

BUTCHERING HISTORY: BIG SCREEN STORYTELLING GONE WRONG

History shmistory— who needs the truth when the embellished version sounds so much more romantic? Life is all too often too boring to make it to the big screen, so these films were beefed up a little... well... maybe more than a little.

• **Edison the Man** (1940)—In this classic historical tale, inventor Thomas Edison pops the question to his girlfriend in a whim of romanticism—he taps the big

question in Morse code on a pipe for her to hear upstairs. Unfortunately, he never did such a thing. Edison did propose to his second wife in Morse code, but it wasn't tapped out on a pipe—he tapped it out on the palm of her hand.

• **Ben-Hur** (1959)—Jesus plays a big role in the underlying plot of this film, but the director forgot to do his math when penciling in his list of minor characters. When Pilate gives word of the upcoming chariot race, he drops a few names of contestants traveling from Corinth and Carthage. However, historically speaking, both of those cities were demolished in 146 BCE—before Jesus was ever born.

- **Braveheart** (1995)—William Wallace may have gone down in history for his famous "Freedom!" scream, but the film about his heroic efforts for the autonomy of Scotland tends to stretch the truth a bit. At the end of the movie, after brave Wallace has been martyred, the Scots rush out to battle the Brits right away. In reality, however, the battle didn't occur until nine years later.

- **Rudy** (1993)—Although the film was set in the mid-1970s, the director seemed to be too lazy to take out references to the 1980s and 1990s. Many of the cars that drive about on set are late model Toyota Corollas and Ford Explorers. In the opening scene, modern streetlights and floodlights line the road. Also, when Rudy goes outside to get his mail, Waddicks Café is in the background—a restaurant that wasn't named "Waddicks" until the 1990s.

★ ★ ★ ★ ★

SITCOMS THAT STUNK: TELEVISION'S WORST SPIN-OFFS

Seinfeld. M*A*S*H*. Cheers. The Brady Bunch. **Some sitcoms touch the American public** so deeply, or make them laugh so uncontrollably, that they go down in history as unforgettable. However, there can be too much of a good thing. These spin-off sitcoms proved that it's not always a good idea to go for Round Two.

AfterMASH
Spin-off of: *M*A*S*H**

Why It Flopped: After a mere fourteen months on the air, every last clip of *AfterMash* hit the cutting room floor. Yep, they got canceled. So why didn't America care for the continuation of war, guns, and medical supplies? Maybe because the show was no longer about war, guns, and medical supplies. Following up from a hit show about a surgical hospital during the Korean War, it just didn't fly when the plotline was moved to the suburbia of Riverbend, Missouri. If that weren't enough, the show's original stars were nowhere to be found. The idea of a spin-off bored them, and three minor characters had to step up to be a part of the new show—Harry Morgan, who played Colonel Potter; William Christopher, who played Father Mulcahy; and Jamie Farr, who played Corporal Klinger. Aside from relocating to the bland deserts of America, *AfterMash* just didn't have the same appeal when Corporal Klinger lost his fetish for dressing in women's clothing. The show's entire plotline conflict had disappeared, and nothing that happens in Missouri could possibly be as exciting as the front lines.

The Bradys
Spin-off of: *The Brady Bunch*

Why It Flopped: Kicked off the air in only one month, *The Bradys* wasn't nearly as captivating as the original sitcom. Maybe the new theme song was getting a little too annoying for veteran viewers, but with the Brady kids grown, the storylines got grim. Instead of chuckling at how cute little Cindy was when she got jealous of her sisters, now the Bradys were juggling alcoholism, HIV, and infertility. Makes being in trouble for breaking the family lamp (and breaking your sister's nose with a football) sound like a trip to the beach. To make things worse, network executives thought they would brighten the gloomy show with canned laughter. It just didn't mesh.

The Ropers
Spin-off of: *Three's Company*
Why It Flopped: Off the air in only one year, *The Ropers* centered around the lives of the landlords of the original show. Mr. Roper was a stubborn, grumpy old man who never seemed to leave the house. Mrs. Roper was a horny woman who, too, never seemed to leave the house. Despite producers trying to spice up interest in their show by tossing in a new female boarder, it just didn't do the trick.

That '80s Show
Spin-off of: *That '70s Show*
Why It Flopped: Almost immediately after its pilot episode, the show's new viewers called in to producers complaining that they didn't get their '80s jokes right. It was one stereotype after another—overkill on clunky shoes, huge telephones, etc. *That '80s Show* was cut after just one season, and unfortunately, most people didn't even notice it was pulled.

★ ★ ★ ★ ★

HOLLYWOOD'S BIGGEST MOVIE BLOOPERS: EDITING GONE WRONG

With all the details that go into making a movie, it's no surprise that every now and then, an oversight leaves room for a few flops in consistency. Check out the following most ridiculous bloopers popular movies have to offer.

- In the animated film *Emperor's New Groove* (2000), Yzma plays on the emperor's throne while her eyelashes magically multiply and disappear. In some shots there are three lashes per eye, in others there are four, five, or six.

- In *King Kong* (1933), Kong trashes the village after Ann escapes from his lair while villagers run for their lives. One villager trips over a chicken cage, and viewers can see his wig falling off his head.

- In *As Good As It Gets* (1997), Carol takes a bus to visit Melvin. As the camera pans out from the scene, however, a sign on the bus reads "Not In Service."

- In *Armageddon* (1998), Harry loses his cool at the oil rig and slams A.J.'s door after pounding it with a golf club, causing a fan to fall to the floor. In the very next shot, however, the fan is back up on the shelf.

- In *Mary Poppins* (1964), Mary powders her nose with black soot before going to explore London's rooftops, but seconds later, her nose is clean again.

- In *10 Things I Hate About You* (1999), Michael has trouble deciding whether he wants the goggles on his helmet up or down. When he visits Kat at her car in the parking lot, they are over his eyes. In the very next shot, they are up on his forehead.

- In *Smokey and the Bandit* (1977), the Bandit sees Carrie and skids, leaving marks on the road that are gone moments later when Cledus's truck passes by.

- In the first two *Austin Powers* flicks, Dr. Evil has brown eyes, but in *Goldmember,* they changed to blue in several scenes.

- In *Dirty Dancing* (1987), as Patrick Swayze's character fights Robbie, his belt switches from being perfectly fastened to broken and dangling—then back to fastened again.

- In *Catch Me If You Can* (2002), the skyline at the LaGuardia Airport shows the Twin Towers. However, the movie is set in 1969, and the Towers weren't built until 1973.

- In *Indiana Jones and the Temple of Doom* (1984), an elephant sprays Indie and Willie with water. Actor Harrison Ford knew it was coming—viewers can see him flinch right before he gets hit.

- In *The Lost World: Jurassic Park* (1997), Jeff Goldblum's character looks through his binoculars backwards at the helicopters, but when the camera cuts to the view, it is zoomed in as if he had looked through them correctly.

- In one of the opening scenes of *A Few Good Men* (1992), the buttons on Tom Cruise's shirt keep appearing as buttoned then unbuttoned. Additionally, a small stain on his shirt appears and disappears more than once.

- In *Save the Last Dance* (2001), Derek (played by actor Sean Patrick Thomas) walks into a restaurant just as one of his buddies says, "What up, Sean!"

★ ★ ★ ★ ★

MOMENTS OF SHAME: AWARD CEREMONIES GONE WRONG

The Academy Award and Golden Globe ceremonies are a time for schmoozing on the red carpet, sashaying around in skimpy skirts, and rubbing Vaseline on your teeth to help fake that perfect paparazzi smile. One would think such an evening would lead to glitz and glamour, but these stars weren't thinking straight when they suddenly embarrassed themselves on their big night.

- In her 2002 Academy Award acceptance speech, actress Halle Berry had to thank just about everyone—her mother, her manager, her husband, and ... her lawyer. "I gotta thank my lawyer Neil

Meyer for making this deal!" she squealed. No one in the audience could believe their ears.

- When Tom Hanks won the Best Actor Academy Award for his work in *Philadelphia*, barely beating costar Denzel Washington for the prize, he sang the praises of Bruce Springsteen and Neil Young

STEAL FROM THE RICH AND GIVE TO THE RICHER

At the 2003 Academy Awards, an expensive goodie basket was handed off to performers, nominees, and presenters at the award show. It included:

- A $1,500 gift card to Morton's Steakhouse
- A $350 cashmere halter top
- A $250 Omas blue pen
- A $3,000 vanity makeup kit
- A $1,000 sampler of Revlon makeup
- A $475 sheet
- A $500 evening bag
- A $15,000 spa package from Estee Lauder

That's just some of the loot. The following year, the estimated total value of the goodie bag jumped to at least $110,000, including tickets to see Celine Dion in Las Vegas, an espresso machine, a seven-day cruise, and a wide-screen television. That's the good news. The bad news is that the freebies qualify as taxable income and must be reported on tax returns.

AWARD-WINNING TRIVIA

- The first Academy Awards ceremony to be telecast was the 25th, in 1953.

- The 1st Academy Awards were presented in 1927.

- Between 1931 and 1969, Walt Disney collected thirty-five Oscars.

- In 1969, *Midnight Cowboy* became the first and only X-rated production to win the Academy Award for Best Picture. Its rating has since been changed to R.

for their work on the film's title track, "Streets of Philadelphia." Referencing his wife, Rita Wilson, and then fellow cast mate Antonio Banderas, Hanks got a little out of control when he referred to Banderas as "second to my lover, is the only person I would trade for." So his wife is not all that bad, but Banderas is a tempting person to cheat with? Hanks should have thought twice.

- In 1999, when actress Sharon Stone was nominated for Best Actress for her work in *The Muse*, USA Films delivered a handful of complimentary Coach watches to the Hollywood Foreign Press Association voters responsible for the outcome of the upcoming Golden Globe Awards. However, once the press caught wind of the apparent bribery (the watches were sent as a gift from Stone), the voters returned the watches. Stone lost the award to *Tumbleweeds* star Janet McTeer.

★ ★ ★ ★ ★

CENSOR ME THIS: SCRIPT SELECTIONS GONE WRONG

CENSOR

Directors will go a long way to make a movie that pushes the envelope or makes people think about a social issue in a new light. However, if it's going to be a shock fest that results in the best parts getting censored, is it really worth the headache? Here are the top four films ever screened by associations and governments worldwide and why they just had to be altered.

Amistad (1997)
Director—Steven Spielberg
Awards—1998 Broadcast Film Critics Association Awards for Best Supporting Actor (Anthony Hopkins)
Cast—Morgan Freeman, Nigel Hawthorne, Anthony Hopkins, Matthew McConaughey, Djimon Hounsou
Summary—The shocking story of the Spanish slave ship *La Amistad*, the film chronicles the painful journey of fifty-three kidnapped native Africans being kept in the cargo hold until they decided to break their shackles and fight for freedom.
Why It Was Censored—Brigham Young University (a Mormon school) probably banned the film because of its excessive nudity. Jamaica's governmental Cinematographic Authority had a sinking feeling *Amistad* was simply too graphic for the locals—especially the scene where the slaves kill the slave traders with machetes. A large percentage of Jamaicans were descendants of West African

slaves at the time, and the government just didn't want the film to pose as an insult to their heritage. They had the bloodiest scenes removed.

The Birth of a Nation (1915, originally titled *The Clansmen*)
Director—D.W. Griffith
Awards—NONE
Cast—Lillian Gish, Mae Marsh, Henry B. Walthall, Miriam Cooper
Summary—Griffith adapted his tale of racism and riots during the Reconstruction of the South from two novels that were all the rage in the early 1900s—*The Clansmen* and *The Leopard's Spots*. One of the books' authors was a Southern preacher whose uncle was a bigwig in the Ku Klux Klan. Needless to say, the plotline, which highlighted a Northern family (the Stonemans) and a Southern family (the Camerons), involved a lot of racial slurs.
Why It Was Censored—The film opens with "A Plea for the Art of the Motion Picture" stating that some viewers may be offended by content, but filmmakers wanted to "show the dark side of wrong, that we may illuminate the bright side of virtue." Initially released in the most popular movie theaters in large cities, *The Birth of a Nation* made big bucks. However, it was highly criticized by the National Association for the Advancement of Colored People, who had previously asked the National Board of Censorship of Motion Pictures to shut down production. After a handful of marches on the state capitol, the governor of Ohio banned the film from his state, as did officials in cities like Denver, Pittsburgh, St. Louis, and Minneapolis. Regardless, an estimated 825,000 people paid to see the flick in 1915 alone.

Pressure for censorship in the movies began in the 1920s, when as many as twenty-two state legislatures considered bills to impose state and local censorship. Hollywood responded in 1922 by establishing the Motion Picture Producers and Distributors of America as an agency to regulate from within what they didn't want regulated from without. The group published its list of "The Don'ts and Be Carefuls" in 1927, which asked them to be careful of such things as those listed below:

• Profanity that included the name of God in any form

• Licentious or suggestive nudity

• Illegal drugs

• Any implication of sexual perversion

• White slavery

• Intimate relationships between races

• Venereal diseases

• Depictions of actual childbirth

• Children's private parts

• Ridicule of the clergy

• Deliberate offense to any race or creed

In addition, special care was directed in such matters as the treatment of the flag, international relations, violent crimes, graphic surgical scenes, cruelty to children and animals, and sympathy for criminals.

La Dolce Vita (1959)

Director—Federico Fellini

Cast—Marcello Mastroianni, Anita Ekberg, Anouk Aimee, Yvonne Furneaux, and Magali Noel

Awards—1961 Academy Award for Best Costume Design, 1961 Cannes Film Festival Golden Palm Award, 1961 New York Film Critics Circle Award for Best Foreign Language Film

Summary—This feisty film follows the life of journalist Marcello Rubini, a man unsatisfied with both his work and his women. Looking for true fulfillment, he explores the life of Roman nightclubs, hookers, and B-list movie stars, hoping for love and a good lead on a story. Although it is credited with coining the word "paparazzi," to some *La Dolce Vita* was nothing more than an exploration of sex and religion.

Why It Was Censored—The Roman Catholic Church banned the flick in most predominantly Catholic parts of the world not because of its sexual prowess but because of the way it criticized its traditional belief system when the main character doubted two girls who claimed to have seen visions of the Virgin Mary. In the U.S., the nudity was written off as art (foreign films always get off the hook for showing skin), but the Catholic Legion of Decency immediately deemed it was only for adults.

Spartacus (1960)

Director—Stanley Kubrick

Cast—Kirk Douglas, Laurence Olivier, Jean Simmons, and Charles Laughton

Awards—1960 Academy Award for Best Art Direction and Set Decoration as well as Best Cinematography and Best Costume Design

Summary—Based on the social condition of Rome before the birth of Christ, *Spartacus* explores a historical slave as he fights as a gladiator for the amusement of the upper class. As Spartacus studies how to be a fighter and an entertainer, he leads an uprising among his fellow slaves, and they fight for their rights as men, husbands, and fathers.

Why It Was Censored—Before the film was even released, some movie critics were in an uproar because *Spartacus* vaguely suggested that protagonist Marcus Crassus was a little light on his feet (he was bisexual). The Production Code Administration had the story line changed and warned that the loincloth costumes better not show too much skin.

Chapter 3

⭐

Rags to Riches:
How Big Stars Earned
Their Keep

Rags to Riches: How Big Stars Earned Their Keep

★ ★ ★ ★ ★ ★ ★ ★ ★ ★ ★ ★ ★ ★ ★ ★

Before they were draped in Chanel petticoats and Louis Vuitton handbags, these A-list celebrities were shacking up in trailers and sleeping on the couches at California comedy clubs. A few million bucks later, now people are paying them to wear the most expensive jewels miners have to offer. These lucky actors have left their former dumpster-diving selves in the dust and are ready to splurge.

CHEESY MOMENTS WITH... JIM CARREY

When he was ten years old, he mailed his resume to *The Carol Burnett Show* to try and get some publicity.

He also wrote letters to rapper Tupac Shakur to cheer him up while he was in jail.

★ ★ ★ ★ ★

JIM CARREY

Best Known For: *In Living Color, Dumb and Dumber,* and *Ace Ventura: Pet Detective*

Humble Beginnings: As a teenager, Carrey's entire family had to take jobs as security officers and janitors at the Titan Wheels Factory just outside of Toronto, Canada. While they lived out of a camper, sixteen-year-old Carrey dropped out of high school to work on his rubber-faced celebrity impersonations and eventually left home to try his hand at the Comedy Store. He worked every night from 1983-1984 in Los Angeles, sleeping on a couch there while he worked on his routine.

Big Break: In 1990, Carrey met comedian Damon Wayans and ended up on the sketch show *In Living Color,* where his eccentric Fire Marshal Bill character would humor some and disturb others who thought his "safety tips" might actually be taken seriously by viewers.

Rollin' in the Dough: As his reputation continued to rise, Carrey wrote himself a $20 million check and set it aside until he made enough to actually cash it. After getting paid for his work in the *The Cable Guy,* he had his dough. Today, Carrey relaxes in a $4.5 million Los Angeles home, a luxurious holiday hotspot in Malibu, and a multimillion-dollar jet. He now requires a cool $25 million per movie.

Little Known Fact: His first wife, Melissa, took him to court because she believed the $10,000 a month he was sending her in child support simply wasn't enough.

★ ★ ★ ★ ★

HILARY SWANK

Best Known For: *The Next Karate Kid* and *Million Dollar Baby*

Humble Beginnings: Swank may have been a high school dropout with a traditional trailer park upbringing, but a hometown role as Mowgli in the play *The Jungle Book* changed everything. Producer and talent scout Suzy Sachs coached her in more small-town roles, but at first, Swank preferred to shine as a local swimmer and gymnast instead. After swimming at the Junior Olympics and ranking fifth in the state for gymastics, she was ready to focus on acting and moved to L.A., with her mother, where they lived out of their car and never looked back.

Big Break: As a teenager, Swank landed cameo roles in the syndicated series *Harry and the Hendersons* and *Growing Pains*, but it was her breakout role as a young judo prodigy in *The Next Karate Kid* that would allow her to use her limber, ex-gymnast ways to climb to fame. After cutting her hair and dressing up as a guy for *Boys Don't Cry* won her an Oscar in 1999, she took her $75/day salary to the mall and broke the bank.

Rollin' in the Dough: In 2002, Swank and husband Chad Lowe— brother of acclaimed actor Rob Lowe—bought a $4 million four-story mansion in Greenwich Village, New York City. In 2004, she signed an exclusive contract with Calvin Klein to pose in the company's classic underwear ads. Today, Swank lives on the edge, often taking time out for skiing, skydiving, and water rafting.

Little Known Fact: On January 15, 2005, Swank was fined $142 plus court costs of $21 for carrying fruit that she didn't declare in customs into New Zealand. She wrote in a letter to the court that "After my twenty-hour flight, I simply forgot I had one orange and one apple. I do apologize sincerely."

★ ★ ★ ★ ★

LINDSAY LOHAN

Best Known For: *The Parent Trap* and *Mean Girls*

Humble Beginnings: Her family may not have had much money in their early years, but at three years old, she helped pay the bills as she supported the family, making more than sixty commercials, including spots for Jell-O, The Gap, and Pizza Hut.

Big Break: Although she was first recognized in Hollywood as Hallie Parker/Annie James in *The Parent Trap*, when Lohan first moved to Los Angeles as a teenager, she shared an apartment with fellow child star Raven Simon. The

two single girls were making plenty of money and had a private maid and chef service in their apartment complex.

Rollin' in the Dough: Lohan has made so much cash between her days as a young, freckle-faced commercial kid and a star-power pop diva-turned-actress that her estranged father has engaged in lengthy court battles to try and get his fair share. Today, Lohan drives a Mercedes-Benz convertible, which she has wrecked multiple times due to the dangerous driving of nosy paparazzi.

Little Known Fact: She is allergic to blueberries, and she used to collect Beanie Babies.

★ ★ ★ ★ ★

MARTIN LAWRENCE

Best Known For: *Bad Boys* and *House Party*

Humble Beginnings: The Lawrence family was wanting when it came to cash. Martin's mother worked multiple retail jobs just to pay the bills, and, in hopes of cheering her up at the end of a long day, Lawrence started telling jokes. At school, it was well known among students and teachers that he had a knack for comedy, but he interrupted so many classroom lectures with smart-aleck remarks that one teacher started helping him get gigs at local clubs, so he would direct his jokes away from the blackboard and toward the proper audience. The early days of stand-up involved some tough crowds who weren't used to his crude humor and language, though— so Lawrence had to supplement his income by cleaning the floors at Sears alongside aspiring rappers Salt-N-Pepa and Kid 'N Play.

Big Break: Like many stars, Lawrence was discovered on *Star Search*, although he was initially afraid that his foul mouth would put off Ed McMahon. Luckily, the host laughed and let him on the show. Lawrence may have headed back to Sears after losing in the last round, but the five minutes of fame got him work:

- 1988—Had a small role on the final season of the sitcom *What's Happening Now!!*

- 1989—Played Cee in the Spike Lee film *Do the Right Thing*

- 1990—Played deejay Bilal in *House Party*

- 1992—Made phrases like "wassup" and "talk to the hand" famous on Fox's *Martin*

Rollin' in the Dough: In 1997, Lawrence made $6 million for his part in *Nothing To Lose*. Six years later, his rate had risen significantly—he made a whopping $20 million for *Bad Boys II*.

Little Known Fact: As a child, Lawrence was so sure that his comedy was funny that one of his teachers agreed to reserve the last five minutes of class for his stand-up routine in exchange for his promise to stop disrupting class with his humor.

★ ★ ★ ★ ★

Oprah Winfrey

Best Known For: *The Oprah Winfrey Show*

Humble Beginnings: Born in a small farm house in rural Mississippi, Winfrey couldn't get a break from her very first breath—her name was spelled wrong on her birth certificate. She would end

up being called Oprah instead
of Orpah (from the Bible), as
her parents intended, and
she spent much of her
childhood working her
grandparents' farm with no
television, no radio, and no
bathroom. She owned two
pairs of shoes. Rebellious in
her youth, she was a lover
of all things naughty and
got in loads of trouble until
her father laid down the law
and, as she says, saved her life.

Big Break: Within months of getting the host spot on, *A.M. Chicago*, the show went from last place in ratings to over taking *Donahue* as the highest rated talk show in Chicago. He encouraged her to leave to further her career, and they are still friends. Her show was then renamed *The Oprah Winfrey Show*—and Winfrey got her riches.

Rollin' In The Dough: A 2005 *Forbes Magazine* report listed Winfrey as worth $1.3 billion. She lives on a 42-acre Oceanside estate in Montecito, California. When she met the original owners at a party early in her career, she reportedly wrote them a check for $50 million on the spot. The house was not for sale, but Winfrey was convincing.

Little Known Fact: Oprah really got her start interviewing her corncob doll and the crows on the fence of her family's property. Her grandmother said she was "on stage" from the minute she could talk.

★ ★ ★ ★ ★

HALLE BERRY

Best Known For:
Monster's Ball and
Catwoman

Humble Beginnings:
Because her parents
divorced when she was
just four years old, Halle Berry was raised by a single mother who
worked as a nurse in the psych unit of a hospital. But the lack of cash
didn't hurt her reputation as might be expected. A prom queen since
high school, Berry won the Miss Teen All-American Pageant in 1985,
and was first runner-up in the Miss
USA Pageant the following year.

Big Break: After trying her hand at
modeling, Berry first hit the big
screen playing an aspiring catwalker
in the 1989 sitcom *Living Dolls*. It
bombed and was soon off the air. It
was her next role as a drug addict in
Jungle Fever that truly put her on the
map.

> A CHEESY MOMENT
> WITH... HALLE BERRY
> Christy Fichtner, the
> contestant who
> beat Berry for the
> Miss USA title in
> 1986, competed on
> the 2003 reality
> show *Who Wants to
> Marry My Dad?*

Rollin' In The Dough: In 2004, she
made $14 million for her work in
Catwoman, and pocketed an extra tip of $500,000 to do her first
topless love scene in the film *Swordfish*.

Little Known Fact: In 2005, Berry became the first actress to actually attend and accept an insulting Razzie Award for her alleged terrible acting in *Catwoman*. Her speech: "When I was a kid, my mother told me that if you could not be a good loser, then there's no way you could be a good winner. Thank you, and I hope to God I never see you guys again."

★ ★ ★ ★ ★

JOHNNY DEPP

Best Known For: *Edward Scissorhands* and *Pirates of the Caribbean*

Humble Beginnings: Born in Kentucky, Depp moved more than thirty times with his parents (sometimes even just to the house next door) before he was even a teenager. His mom, who is part Cherokee, bought him a guitar when he was thirteen years old, and two years later, desperate to be a rock and roll star, he dropped out of school to make it big with his band, The Kids. They thought they had hit the big time when they landed gigs opening for Iggy Pop, but the band broke up after tensions mounted when Depp married

A CHEESY MOMENT WITH...
JOHNNY DEPP
Johnny Depp wanted to cap some of his teeth in gold for his role as the comical pirate Captain Jack Sparrow in *Pirates of the Caribbean: The Curse of the Black Pearl*, but he had a sneaking suspicion that his director and producers would disagree. To make room for a compromise, he had most of his teeth capped then agreed to get rid of some of them (but not all) before taping began.

one of his band mate's little sisters. Desperate for cash, Depp worked as a telemarketer (selling pens), and his wife, Lori Anne Allison, was a makeup artist.

Big Break: Heeding some hardy advice he got from actor Nicolas Cage, whom he met on a trip to Los Angeles, Depp decided to support his family with Hollywood dollars and made it big when he landed a role as an undercover cop on *21 Jump Street*.

Rollin' In The Dough: He spent $350,000 revamping a Los Angeles nightclub and dubbed it the Viper Room, beating out similar bids made by Arnold Schwarzenegger, who also had hoped to make the buy. Depp also bought his very own tropical island in 2004.

Little Known Fact: Depp is an underground musician and has recorded with British band Oasis on more than one occasion. He plays the slide guitar on the 1997 album *Be Here Now*.

★ ★ ★ ★ ★

MARY TYLER MOORE

Best Known For: *The Mary Tyler Moore Show*

Humble Beginnings: The humble winner of seven Emmy Awards, life wasn't always so sweet for actress Mary Tyler Moore. She started out in Hollywood as an elf that danced around appliances in a General Electric commercial that aired during the 1955 *Ozzie and Harriet* show. Moore's first reoccurring role was a small part on *Richard Diamond, Private Detective*, but producers never showed her face. Moore's life would later include a series of personal tragedies— her son accidentally shot and killed himself, her sister committed suicide, and her last living sibling died of cancer.

Big Break: Moore's major breakout role was as Laura Petrie, the wife of a New York comedy writer, in *The Dick Van Dyke Show*. Although struggling with a drinking problem like costar Van Dyke, she sobered up and went on to win an Academy Award nomination for her work in the film *Ordinary People*, which was the first time she stepped away from her lighthearted persona as an actress.

Rollin' in the Dough: In 1970, Moore and her then husband formed MTM Enterprises. This production company produced many hit TV series, including *The Mary Tyler Moore Show, Rhoda, The Bob Newhart Show, WKRP in Cincinnati,* and *Hill Street Blues.* Moore maintains a ritzy apartment on the Upper East Side of Manhattan.

Little Known Fact: Today, a statue of Moore sits in downtown Minneapolis near the Nicollet Mall in honor of her role as the quirky thirty-something news reporter from *The Mary Tyler Moore Show*.

★ ★ ★ ★ ★

RICHARD GERE

Best Known For: *Pretty Woman* and *An Officer and a Gentleman*

Humble Beginnings: Richard Gere grew up with his extended family on a demure dairy farm and stuck around small-town settings while he studied at the University of Massachusetts Amherst on a gymnastics

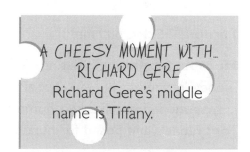

A CHEESY MOMENT WITH...
RICHARD GERE
Richard Gere's middle name is Tiffany.

scholarship. A few back handsprings later, he decided to leave the gym and instead pursue two new careers—acting and playing the trumpet.

Big Break: After wowing British crowds as hot rod racer Danny Zuko in the 1973 play *Grease*, he landed a role as a male prostitute in *American Gigolo* (1980), in which he made designer Armani famous with his dashing good looks. Gere hasn't stopped wooing women onscreen since, earning him a coveted 1999 election as *People* magazine's sexiest man alive.

Rollin' In The Dough: The winner of multiple Golden Globe Awards over the years, Gere's talent and good looks are so well known that he was actually stalked in 2002 by a crazed fan who called him more than a thousand times. She would leave him haunting voicemails saying, "I will follow you" and "I want to be with you and share your life."

Little Known Fact: Gere was the first man ever to have his picture on the cover of *Vogue* magazine (with wife Cindy Crawford in the early 1990s). Since then, George Clooney has been the only other actor to have that honor.

★ ★ ★ ★ ★

KIM BASINGER

Famous Flicks: *Batman*

Humble Beginnings: Basinger's family may not have had much money in their early years, but after she won the Junior Miss competition in her Georgia hometown, she signed a contract with Ford Models and posed for hundreds of print advertisements. When she left to pursue her acting dreams (and more cash) in the fall of 1971, her father wished her well with some cash and a locket that read, "Today a Star, Tomorrow a Superstar."

Big Break: Although her first sitcom, *Dog and Cat,* was canceled without even completing its first season, Basinger demanded the attention of every man in America when in 1982 she became one of the first actresses to pose in *Playboy.* She went on to become the legendary Bond girl Domino in *Never Say Never Again*, and she hasn't stopped bringing in the riches since.

Rollin' in the Dough: In 1989, Basinger paid $20 million for the town of Braselton, Georgia, in hopes of making it a tourist attraction with a popular new film festival. Unfortunately, she had to sell it when business went bad in 1993.

Little Known Fact: She once wrote a letter to the U.S. Agriculture Secretary insisting that the mistreatment of circus animals in America has got to stop. The actress had heard a story about a baby

elephant in the Ringling Bros. and Barnum & Bailey Circus who was forced to perform while it was sick. The elephant died, and Basinger got on her soapbox.

★ ★ ★ ★ ★

ROSIE O'DONNELL

Famous Flicks: *Sleepless in Seattle* and *A League of Their Own*

Humble Beginnings: As a high school student in Long Island, Rosie wasn't the richest kid at school—but she sure was popular. Her peers voted her class president, homecoming queen, and prom queen. Increasingly popular for her boyish looks and her heavyset midriff, she started piecing together a living doing stand-up along the East Coast.

> **A CHEESY MOMENT WITH...**
> **ROSIE O'DONNELL**
> Rosie O'Donnell was such a fan of the hit show *Who Wants to Be a Millionaire?* that she got on a fan's lifeline list and helped brainstorm the correct answer to the $32,000 question.

Big Break: O'Donnell's comedy act was discovered by Claudia McMahon (the daughter of popular *Star Search* host Ed McMahon), who convinced her to audition for the show. Rosie held the voters' top spot for five weeks and made $20,000 off the project. Later, she hosted VH1's comedy series *Stand-Up Spotlight* and never looked back.

Rollin' In The Dough: O'Donnell recently put her money where her mouth is and paired up with partner Kelli Carpenter to start R Family Vacations, a cruise line to the Bahamas specifically for gay families. The highlight of the trip—discussion groups on artificial insemination, surrogacy, and adoption.

Little Known Fact: She shares a birthday with Matthew Broderick, collects Happy Meal toys, and loves the band Savage Garden.

O'Donnell also refuses to sign autographs for anyone older than a teenager.

★ ★ ★ ★ ★

BEFORE THEY WERE STARS... EARLY NOT-SO-GLAMOUROUS JOBS

- Ashton Kutcher worked at a Cheerios factory in Iowa.

- Shemp Howard of *The Three Stooges* was an apprentice to a plumber.

- *Saturday Night Live*'s Phil Hartman was a graphic designer.

- Brad Pitt dressed up in a giant chicken suit to advertise outside Mexican restaurant El Pollo Loco when he first moved to Los Angeles. He made just over $3 an hour.

- Funnyman Andy Dick worked as a tour guide and directed commercials for the Utah Transit Authority before making his big screen debut in *In the Army Now* with Pauly Shore.

- Comedian Bob Hope was a boxer.

- After high school, Ellen Degeneres worked shucking oysters, painting houses, and bartending.

- *Gilligan's Island* star Bob Denver got a degree in political science from Los Angeles Loyola University and was a teacher in California in the 1950s.

- *Home Improvement*'s Richard Karn (Al Borland) was the superintendent of an apartment complex.

- Edgy comedian Chris Rock worked at Red Lobster.

- Keanu Reeves sharpened ice skates.

- Whoopi Goldberg worked as a beautician at a funeral home—putting makeup on dead bodies.

★ ★ ★ ★ ★

BEFORE THEY WERE STARS... EARLY GIGS

- Denzel Washington played a nervous doctor on *St. Elsewhere*, an award-winning 1980s medical drama.

- *60 Minutes* interviewer Mike Wallace was a game show host for *The Big Surprise, Who's The Boss?*, and *Guess Again* in the 1950s.

- In the early 1980s, George Clooney shot pilots for fifteen different failed sitcoms and had small roles in six other sitcoms, including *The Facts of Life*.

- Leonardo DiCaprio played a homeless boy taken in for the holidays by the Seaver family on *Growing Pains*.

- Jim Carrey was a cartoonist for the 1984 sitcom *The Duck Factory*, but it went off the air after just a few months.

- In 1982 Demi Moore played a reporter on *General Hospital*.

- Jennifer Lopez got her start dancing as a Fly Girl on *In Living Color*.

- Salma Hayek's first American gig was a recurring role on *The Sinbad Show* in 1993.

- Ryan Phillippe played the first openly gay adolescent daytime TV had ever seen on *One Life to Live.*

Don't Quit Your Day Job: Actors Who Tried Their Hand at Singing

These leading Hollywood men may have been desperate to make a buck before they landed roles in blockbuster flicks, but they should have never passed time behind the microphone.

- Keanu Reeves: Played bass in a grunge band called Dogstar that put out two albums.

- Russell Crowe: Sang in the group 30 Odd Foot of Grunts.

- William Shatner: Put out several spoken-word songs including a cover of "Lucy in the Sky with Diamonds" and the single "Common People," which, despite its terrible lyrics and melody, have gained a cult following similar to that of *American Idol* wannabe William Hung.

- David Hasselhoff: A huge pop star in Germany, he has put out seven solo albums since the 1980s.

- Billy Bob Thornton: Singer and drummer who played countless covers of Creedence Clearwater Revival songs with his buddies in high school and released his first album, *Private Radio*, in 2001.

- Bruce Willis: Wasted two decades putting out his version of classics, which sold millions.

Chapter 4

✩

Embarrassing Celebrity Scandals

Embarrassing Celebrity Scandals

★ ★ ★ ★ ★ ★ ★ ★ ★ ★ ★ ★ ★ ★ ★ ★

There's something fishy going on amidst the Hollywood red carpet, and mum's been the word for too long. Here are the secrets behind the greatest stories your favorite celebrity mischief-makers have to offer. From a talk show host hooking up with his stripper guest to a drunken actor passing out in a stranger's bed, these superstars are nothing but trouble.

TIDBITS OF GARY COLEMAN TRIVIA

He sued his parents for "misappropriating" $8.3 million while he was a child actor, and in 1993 won a $1.28 million settlement.

In 1999, after his entrepreneurship for a California video game arcade flopped, he filed for bankruptcy and got a job as a security guard at the mall.

He was a candidate for governor in the 2003 California election and was voted as the eighth most likely winner (out of 135 possible candidates).

★ ★ ★ ★ ★

COOKIE MONSTER MISBEHAVES

When a theme park brings in the cast of *Sesame Street* for the week, business is bound to be good. **But when the characters start roughing up the children**, you know it's going to be a long day. One such park in Langhorne, Pennsylvania, suffered this sad fate when a pushy father asked Cookie Monster to pose for a photo with his daughter. The character allegedly put his "big blue paw" on the little girl's head and gave her a shove. Whether it was an act of aggression or simply an encouraging pat gone wrong, the girl's father got rowdy and assaulted the monster in return, kicking and shoving him repeatedly. Needless to say, he was arrested, and hundreds of children—who had just helplessly watched their furry blue friend get tackled to the ground—had a good cry.

★ ★ ★ ★ ★

SNUB ME UP, SCOTTY

William Shatner has long been known for his brave façade—he narrated hundreds of life-saving moments on *Rescue 911* and demonstrated stern-faced leadership on *Star Trek*, didn't he? Regardless of his heroic reputation, Shatner was in for a shock when he found out that many of his costars thought he was a total snob. While contacting the old cast of *Star Trek* to interview them for his memoir, *Star Trek Memories*, he uncovered the fact that everyone who worked with him on the set thought he was rude, distant, and disinterested. Upset that he had come across so uncouth, Shatner tried to organize a reunion to patch up old wounds and reminisce on good times, but one famous face—James Doohan, who played "Scotty"—refused to attend.

★ ★ ★ ★ ★

DID YOU KNOW

In 2003, William Shatner's version of "Lucy in the Sky with Diamonds" was voted one of the worst "massacres" of a Beatles single ever.

DIRTY LAUNDRY: THE SECRET LIFE OF TALK SHOW HOSTS

The world of daytime talk shows is a circus of crude confessions and scandalous paternity tests, but the lives of those mysterious men behind the microphone have a few trashy secrets of their own.

- **Montel Williams**

  Montel graduated from the United States Naval Academy in Annapolis, Maryland, with a degree in General Engineering. Sounds like an intelligent, respectable man, right? Not so fast. A few weeks after the breakout of his new talk show *Montel*, he actually "fell in love" with one of the guests from the shocking "Mother-Daughter Strippers" episode. The two ended up getting married, and Grace, known as Bambi Jr. on the job at several hot Las Vegas hotels, consulted a psychic to see if the two were really compatible. The relationship didn't last.

- **Geraldo**

    Whether it's a glimpse into his personal life or the many places he takes the camera, controversy has always seemed to follow Geraldo Rivera. In high school, he joined a gang and got busted stealing a car. In college, he got married to postpone his chances of getting drafted into the Vietnam War. It was during an early job at WABC in New York, however, that would seal his boldness (and stupidity) as a journalist in history—while taping a story about how easy it is to obtain heroin on the street, he bought a bump (which is a felony). After a brief suspension, no charges were formally filed.

- **Dr. Phil**

    Texas television psychologist Phil McGraw was in hot water after a few former fans accused his  "Shape Up!" diet and exercise plan of being completely useless. McGraw's book, they said, instructed them to take twenty-two herbal supplements and vitamins that have put a damper on their monthly budget. The weight didn't come off as expected, so they sought out for cash in court instead.

★ ★ ★ ★ ★

WHATCHOO ANGRY ABOUT, GARY?

Ever the master of wisdom with wit, Gary Coleman—the short-but-feisty star of *Diff'rent Strokes*—went a little overboard when a woman asked for his autograph while he was working as a security guard at the mall. She accused him of throwing a punch, and he was arrested under misdemeanor assault and battery charges. Coleman told the jury that he thought he was in danger—the woman was taller than him and had been spouting off insults about his talent (or lack thereof). In the end, however, he pleaded "no contest," spent ninety days in jail and paid a measly small fine. After a few rounds of anger-management classes, he shelled out more cash to pay off the woman's hospital bills and continued with his struggle to keep his name out of the headlines.

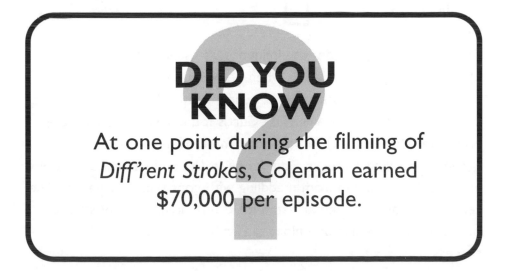

DID YOU KNOW

At one point during the filming of *Diff'rent Strokes*, Coleman earned $70,000 per episode.

Since then, Coleman has been known to frequently lose his cool. While filming a cameo appearance on the celebrity has-been reality show *The Surreal Life*, he lost it again when rapper Vanilla Ice got nearly everyone in a restaurant to beg him to spout off his famous lines "Whatchoo talkin' 'bout, Willis?" He lashed out in embarrassment, quit the show, and called a cab. Talk about good reality TV.

★ ★ ★ ★ ★

NAPPING WITH NARCOTICS

You know tomorrow is going to be a bad day when the paparazzi catch you snoozing in a stranger's bed. In July 1997, a thirty-one-year-old Robert Downey Jr. (under the influence, as usual) got his face plastered all over the tabloids when he wandered about Malibu, trespassed on a neighbor's property, and eventually passed out in the bedroom. When homeowner Lisa Curtis found a stranger snoozing under her sheets, she called the cops and Downey went to jail (again). A budding career in *Saturday Night Live* and *Natural Born Killers* just couldn't keep him from meddling with controlled substances. The year before, he had been arrested for drunk driving and possession of heroin, cocaine, and an unloaded revolver—not a recipe for success.

★ ★ ★ ★ ★

In Living Trouble

Always known as one of the edgiest potty-mouth comedians to step on stage, Martin Lawrence was in true form in 1996 when police chased him down for running into a busy Los Angeles intersection and waving a gun at passing cars. It turns out he was suffering from a serious case of anxiety. Cops (and doctors) decided he was depressed, dehydrated, and in need of a good night's sleep. Just a few months later, Lawrence was in trouble again after authorities found a pistol on him at Burbank Airport. This time he couldn't get off by saying he was in desperate need of a nap. In fact, Lawrence has spent the rest of his career explaining away similar shady "incidents":

- His wife accused him of being verbally abusive, took out a restraining order, hired a bodyguard, and then divorced him in 1996.

- *Martin* costar Tisha Campbell filed a sexual harassment lawsuit against him and threatened to quit the show unless producers promised she would never have to tape a scene with him again.

- He was questioned and arrested after a fight broke out in a nightclub in 1997.

★ ★ ★ ★ ★

SWIMMIN' POOLS... MOVIE STARS... GET A LAWYER...

Originally scripted as *The Hillbillies of Beverly Hills*, CBS's **The Beverly Hillbillies had legal woes right out of the gate.** As soon as the show became popular, a four-man musical group who called themselves The Beverly Hillbillies filed a $2 million suit against Filmways Pictures for copying their namesake. Not long after they settled out of court, writer Hamilton Morgan accused the show's writers of plagiarism and filed a $15 million suit explaining that he had previously been turned down by CBS for his script titled *Country Cousins*, which was remarkably similar to *The Beverly Hillbillies*. A hung jury led to the charges being dismissed, but even after the show went off the air, producers suffered another headache when even more people filed a suit—this time claiming they owned the 1921 Hillbilly flatbed truck and wanted it back. The allegations were proved false, and the beloved truck was shipped to be on permanent display in a museum at the Missouri School of the Ozarks.

DID YOU KNOW

A former back-up singer for Gene Autry and Bing Crosby, Jerry Scoggins sang the theme song for *The Beverly Hillbillies*.

HILLBILLY LINGO

Because it may have been hard to understand exactly what the Clampett family was a-sayin' on their weekly program *The Beverly Hillbillies*, here are their most popular phrases revealed:

- Slippery as a hog on ice
- Feelin' lower than a well digger's heel
- Fine as a frog's hair
- It ain't hern, it's hisn

★ ★ ★ ★ ★

OPRAH GETS OSTRACIZED

The staff at *Ladies Home Journal* isn't much of a fan of Oprah Winfrey and her liberal counseling ways. In fact, the magazine's ex-editor-in-chief, Myrna Blyth, dissed the talk show queen for touting off what she calls feminism and bad advice in the book *Spin Sisters: How the Women of the Media Sell Unhappiness—and Liberalism—to the Women of America.* For example, Blyth believes Winfrey's shows about marital problems focus on cheating men and their poor, pitiful wives rather than noting that oftentimes women are the ones who taint their relationships. She isn't alone in her criticism—others believe that the show's book club is a joke. While it oftentimes brings up big names like Hemingway and Faulkner, other highlights have little literary value. Just ask author Jonathan Franzen, who wished that Winfrey had not chosen his book, *The Corrections*, because he thought her womanpower ways would doom the chances of a man ever picking it up again. There's also that unfortunate James

Frey situation. His popular novel, *A Million Little Pieces,* was lavishly praised on her show until it was revealed that the work was largely fiction, instead of autobiographical as he had insisted.

★ ★ ★ ★ ★

SHE'S DARING, DARLING

Known for her love of short-lived marriages, snappy wit, and calling just about everyone "darling," Hungarian-born actress Zsa Zsa Gabor doesn't always use common sense when it comes to complying with the law. In June 1989, cops flagged her down for speeding in Beverly Hills—but instead of hitting the curb, she panicked and sped off. When she finally obliged and pulled over three blocks away, Gabor was shocked that the policeman actually had the audacity to write her (a rich snob) a ticket. To make sure she clearly communicated her disgust, she smacked him across the face. The speeding ticket cost Gabor a hefty fine, and the slap cost her jail time.

THE MANY HUSBANDS OF ZSA ZSA GABOR

Burhan Belge	1937-1941	Writer, diplomat, and press director for Turkey's foreign ministry
Conrad Hilton	1942-1946	Hilton Hotel mogul
George Sanders	1949-1954	Actor who later married Gabor's sister, Magda.
Herbert Hutner	1964-1966	Financial consultant
Joshua S. Cosden Jr.	1966-1967	Oil heir
Jack Ryan	1975-1976	Inventor of the Chatty Cathy doll
Michael O'Hara	1977-1982	Attorney
Felipe de Alba	1982-1982	Actor, however, the ceremony wasn't valid because she was still married to O'Hara at the time.
Frederick Prinz von Anhalt	1986	German who claims to be a prince because as an adult, he was adopted by a princess.

★ ★ ★ ★ ★

THE WORD OF THE DAY: FREAK!

When Pee Wee Herman (actor Paul Reubens) was visiting his folks in Sarasota, Florida, in the summer of 1991, he decided to go out for a late-night flick—an X-rated flick, that is. A few hours later, he was arrested for "exposing himself" in the theater (which has since been replaced with a restaurant). In no time, every gray-suited Pee Wee doll was pulled from the shelves of toy stores across the nation, and CBS dropped the five remaining episodes of his children's program, *Pee Wee's Playhouse*. Surprisingly, Herman's fellow actors weren't offended—they were supportive. The following September, he got a standing ovation at the MTV Video Music Awards when he acted ignorant of the fact that he had been the butt of Hollywood's jokes. He simply asked the crowd, "Heard any good jokes lately?" They thought he was hilarious.

★ ★ ★ ★ ★

PLAYING NICE WITH NATURE

Leonardo DiCaprio and crew found themselves in a sticky situation in 1999 while filming the tropical flick *The Beach* in Thailand. Apparently, they had a bit of a problem playing nice with nature. The entire time the cast was filming, the set was bombarded by protestors claiming that they had destroyed Phi Phi Leh island's Maya Beach. Native plants had been ripped up, the beach had been plowed, and new palm trees and colorful foliage had been brought in

instead. Local environmentalists called the makeover "sinful," but producers said they were simply doing what was necessary to make their flick as accurate as possible.

★ ★ ★ ★ ★

RATHER'S NASTY RUN-IN

In 1986, two mysterious men made headlines when they attacked CBS anchorman Dan Rather on New York City's Park Avenue and asked him one question over and over—"Kenneth, what's the frequency?" Confused and intimidated, Rather had no clue what they were talking about and didn't know what to say in return. Because of his silence, however, he got the crap beat out of him. When the story broke, many people didn't know whether or not to believe it. Rock band R.E.M. even released a hit song based on the event, titled "What's the Frequency, Kenneth?"

★ ★ ★ ★ ★

BRENDA'S BAD HUMOR

Beverly Hills, 90210 star **Shannen Doherty has long criticized her fans for not being able to separate her real personality with the irritable**, controlling Brenda she embodied for several years on the show. In fact, fans of *90210* even circulated an *I HATE BRENDA* newsletter across the country. However, Doherty's track record with the law reveals that she just might have a problem with keeping her cool.

- August 1992—She lost much of her sitcom earnings and two of her cars when she was sued by California United Bank for writing bad checks. She ended up so broke that she agreed to appear in a Slaughter music video to make some extra cash.

- December 1992—She was charged with battery after getting into a fist fight with another young actress at Hollywood's Roxbury club.

- 1993—Her landlord filed a lawsuit saying she owed him $14,000 in unpaid rent and $100,000 for the damage done to the apartment during a violent fight with her boyfriend.

- August 1996—She threw a bottle through the windshield of a college student's car and was charged with assault with a deadly weapon.

- December 2000—She was arrested for drunken driving, had to pay a $1,500 fine, and agreed to speak to teens about the dangers of alcohol as a community service project.

★ ★ ★ ★ ★

BERRY'S BIG BUMP

On February 23, 2000, **Hollywood bombshell Halle Berry was accused of running a red light** in a rental car, hitting another vehicle, then speeding off in a panic. Though the incident was clearly a hit and run, someone must have felt sorry about the twenty stitches she had to endure at the hospital after she fled. In the end, Berry pleaded "no contest," paid $14,000 in fines, and did two hundred hours of community service.

★ ★ ★ ★ ★

BACHELOR BOB'S BIG BREAK MISTAKE

The chubby comedian from *The Bachelorette*, **Bob Guiney, found himself in a bit of trouble** when he broke contract and tried to launch his music career right after his big moment on the reality show aired on ABC. He had allegedly signed an exclusivity clause with the network that prevented him from promoting other products without an OK from producers. Guiney used his newfound fame to push his new album, *3 Sides*, anyway and wound up in court.

★ ★ ★ ★ ★

THE REAL PASSION OF MEL GIBSON

In a story that stunned those who had seen Mel Gibson's *Passion of the Christ* as a return to religion and traditional values, **the actor was arrested on July 28, 2006, in Malibu,**

California, on suspicion of driving under the influence of alcohol.

A press release from the Los Angeles County Sheriff's Department indicated that Gibson was pulled over after "deputies were alerted by their radar that his speed was above the posted limit." Approaching deputies noted the strong odor of alcohol, and a subsequent Breathalyzer test showed that his blood-alcohol level to be 0.12; the California legal limit is 0.08.

When taken to the station, Gibson launched into an anti-Semetic tirade laced heavily with profanity and sexist remarks for good measure. Although he was not officially charged with DUI—that call will be made by the district attorney—Gibson faced an avalanche of ill will, not the least of which came from Jewish groups that claimed he had expressed his true feelings during the rant.

Gibson admitted that "I disgraced myself," and offered numerous apologies and confessions of guilt to everyone from religious groups to the deputies who arrested him. Then he entered a rehab center for the drinking problem that had plagued him even since the early years of his career.

★ ★ ★ ★ ★

Just Picking Up a Few Things

Actress Winona Ryder was shopping in the Saks Fifth Avenue store in the upscale shopping district of Wilshire Boulevard in December of

2001 when something unexpected happened: **she was arrested for stealing** after security guards suspected her of taking clothing and hair accessories.

Through her attorney, Ms. Ryder said there had been a misunderstanding – she had simply been carrying clothes between departments within the store. But police felt sure of their suspicions, since they based them on a surveillance tape in which the actress was seen removing tags from the store items. Beverly Hills police also said she was carrying drugs for which she did not have a prescription.

She was later acquitted of burglary, but convicted of grand theft and vandalism for stealing $5,560.40 worth of designer merchandise. She was sentenced to three years probation and 480 hours of community service. At the completion of the latter, she was praised by the judge for her behavior during probation.

★ ★ ★ ★ ★

HUGH'S DEVINE ENCOUNTER

There's an old saying that it doesn't matter what they print about you as long as they spell your name right. That certainly turned out to be the case for Hugh Grant, British star of movies like *Nine Months* and *Two Weeks Notice*.

On June 27, 1995, **Grant was arrested for being found in his car, engaged in a sex act with a Hollywood prostitute** named Devine Brown. He was charged with lewd conduct, and was later fined $1,180 and placed on two years' probation.

People wondered why Hugh would have been involved in such action since his long-standing girlfriend was the beautiful Elizabeth

Hurley. Other than that, the most amazing thing about the incident was the way Hugh faced up to it. Within just days of the arrest, he spoke publicly about the whole thing, telling Jay Leno, "I think you know in life what's a good thing to do and what's a bad thing, and I did a bag thing...and there you have it."

Chapter 5

★

The Antics of Acting Animals

The Antics of Acting Animals

★ ★ ★ ★ ★ ★ ★ ★ ★ ★ ★ ★ ★ ★ ★ ★ ★

French writer Romain Rolland once said, "I know at last what distinguishes man from animals: financial worries." He was right on the money. When it comes to bringing in big bucks for doing things like napping and trotting across screen, these pampered pets have made it big in Hollywood. But don't be too impressed. You may be surprised at some of their untold stories from the set.

DID YOU KNOW?

The Benji dog from the latest film, *Off the Leash!*, was "discovered" at an animal shelter in Gulfport, Mississippi.

★ ★ ★ ★ ★

BOARS THAT WON'T GET LOST

When the cast of the sci-fi goes-tropical television series *Lost* filmed the Season One episode "Walkabout," **the plan was for a pack of boars to get chased out of the airplane wreckage** when bad-boy Sawyer found them feeding on the rotten corpses. To manage the rowdy animals, producers brought in a real boar wrangler, but things went awry when the animals refused to cooperate. The wrangler had planned to coax the boars into running across the set by jogging ahead of them with food. However, the extras on set had fed them so many snacks that day that their bellies were full, and they had no interest in the jog at all.

NOT SO SPECIAL EFFECTS

To prepare for a camera shot of a giant white polar bear attacking castaways in one of the first episodes of *Lost*, the crew skipped out on handling a real animal, and instead attached a giant stuffed bear to a wire and swung it past the camera. For shots of the bear running through the jungle, a crewman put on some white furry pants and ran through the trees himself.

★ ★ ★ ★ ★

THE DOG WHO COULDN'T DIE (UNTIL HE DID)

Boasting a loveable pooch with the courage of a lion, **the 1974 blockbuster *Benji* was never expected to be a hit**. However, the brave little dog that rescued kidnapped children in between naps made a whopping $40 million in the United States alone. Two sequels and four prime-time television specials later, few viewers realized that Benji was not one talented pup, but four. After watching *Lady and the Tramp*, writer Joe Camp, the mastermind behind the series, came up with his idea for the family-friendly doggie flick and embarked on a seemingly endless search for a cute little puppy to play the lead role. He searched animal shelters across the country, and finally found the perfect Benji.

★ ★ ★ ★ ★

ANOTHER DOG WHO BIT THE DUST

Unfortunately for the cast and crew of *The Brady Bunch*, **fluffy family dog Tiger was hit by a car and killed early in the taping of the show's first season**. When a replacement dog wouldn't cooperate on set, producers decided to write the pooch out of the script and only bring him in for an occasional cameo. This worked for a while, but it wasn't long before the replacement Tiger got tossed a pink slip in lieu of a Frisbee. Regardless of the fact that a dog would never again grace the Brady home, the doghouse remained throughout every season because it covered holes in the artificial backyard.

★ ★ ★ ★ ★

FROM THE GARBAGE PAIL TO GREEN PAL

With an official celebrated birthday (May 9, 1955) and an honorary doctorate of "Amphibious Letters" from Southampton College (he gave the commencement speech the same day he gave his acceptance speech), **Kermit the Frog is one of the most famous amphibians of all time**. One of puppeteer Jim Henson's most famed figures, Kermit hasn't always been so glamorous and pampered. In fact, the original vision for Kermit's design came from a bunch of garbage—a dirty green jacket Henson found in the trash and two eyes made out of old Ping-Pong balls. Not only was Kermit once ratty and in need of a serious dry cleaning, he was also supposed to be a lizard. He didn't appear as a frog until the 1969 television special *Hey, Cinderella!*, but Kermit's extreme makeover was a hit, and Henson hasn't turned back since. So just how did a stuffed amphibian rise above the likes of Miss Piggy and Fozzie Bear to steal the show as Henson's premier puppet? He was simply the lightest, making him easier to operate for long periods of taping.

WHAT'S WITH THE NAME?

It was once rumored that Kermit the Frog was named after Sesame Street Muppet designer Kermit Love; however, Henson named Kermit while drawing sketches of the character at just eight years old—long before he ever met Love. Others say the frog gets its name from Theodore Kermit Scott, one of Henson's boyhood friends.

COWABUNGA, DUDE!

Kermit's not the only famous green friend. In fact, here's a quartet of them, the Teenage Mutant Ninja Turtles. The story behind them goes like this: In 1984, Kevin Eastman was a college kid dying to impress his roommate with his cartoons of turtles with mighty cool headbands. A comic book junkie, Eastman and his friend Peter Laird put out a black and white version of their drawings, which soon morphed into a hit television show and three movies. Eastman took his fortune and decided to stay in the comic book biz. He bought the rights to *Heavy Metal*, an adult comic book magazine famed for its big-busted drawings of women wearing little clothing. In 1993, he married *Penthouse* hottie Julie Strain and partnered with her to make the film *Heavy Metal 2000*, based on his comics.

★ ★ ★ ★ ★

THE WOOKIE'S WHEEDLE

An overwhelming amount of problems plagued director George Lucas and his colleagues as they worked on creating a "galaxy far, far away" for the film *Star Wars* in the 1970s—they were running out of money, their robots kept breaking down on the set, and there were rumors around Hollywood that the film would turn out to be a children's flick instead of a sci-fi blockbuster. However, one thing bugged producers more than anything—the Wookie wasn't wearing any pants. Along with actors Mark Hamill and Harrison Ford, Lucas could not believe they were wasting their time arguing over such a "bare" issue.

★ ★ ★ ★ ★

What's with the Voice? The Many Mouths of Mickey

No male can hit his falsetto like the famed cartoon Mickey Mouse. In fact, Mickey's high-pitch, friendly voice is part of what makes him so approachable and appealing to children. Walt Disney prided

Why the Gloves?

Walt Disney decided to add white gloves to Mickey Mouse's hands so audiences could distinguish his fingers—and so his arms and hands did not disappear when they laid flat against his body in early black and white versions of the cartoon.

himself on personally recording the voice of Mickey for 19 years, but by 1946, his voice had become so raspy from chain-smoking cigarettes that he could no longer do the part. After one last taping for *Mickey and the Beanstalk*, he passed the torch to fellow animation specialist Jim MacDonald. Today, Wayne Allwine serves as Mickey's pipes, and his wife, voiceover specialist Russi Taylor, is the voice of Mickey's first love, Minnie.

Why the Big Fuss?

Mickey Mouse has stirred up quite a bit of trouble outside the United States in his day. In 1935, Romanian authorities insisted that children would be scared of the giant mouse and banned the videos from being played in movie theaters across their country. The following year, Nazi Germany's Adolf Hitler declared Mickey an official "enemy of the state."

★ ★ ★ ★ ★

BIG BIRD'S TALL TALES

A giant, golden-feathered puppet who promotes goodwill through sharing and saying please and thank you, Big Bird has caused quite a stir in children's television for his long list of lies. First, young viewers everywhere were confused when Big Bird

DID YOU KNOW?

Although Big Bird (played by actress Caroll Spinney) could roller skate, ice skate, write poetry, and ride a unicycle, producers at Sesame Street deemed him only six years old.

made a special appearance in the *Mister Rogers' Neighborhood* Land of Make Believe and proceeded to tell X the Owl that he was a golden condor. However, for years, the bird (by the prompting of his producers) had been describing himself as a giant canary. Next, there was an issue about Mr. Snuffleupagus, whom most of the other characters believed to be imaginary because he only came along when Big Bird was alone. The elusive friend was modeled in part on imaginary

WHAT'S IN THE NEST?

The children's book *Sesame Street Unpaved* reveals that Big Bird keeps the following trinkets in his nest:

- A feather duster
- A record player
- A photo of friend Mr. Hooper
- A bubble gum dispenser
- An umbrella
- A mailbox
- A pair of snowshoes
- A lava lamp
- A football helmet
- A clock (with no hands)
- A watering can
- A tricycle wheel
- A golf bag (with only one club in it)
- A megaphone
- A Roman bust

friends that many of the show's viewers created. Many adults believed that Big Bird used "Snuffy" as a scapegoat to excuse unexplainable mishaps, which tapped into the issue of believing sometimes incredible truths that children say. Creators of the show considered all of these factors against a backdrop of stories where children had not been believed when they reported incidents of abuse and assault that only they had witnessed. In the end, Snuffy was proven to be real, the other characters apologized for their unbelief, and all was well on Sesame Street.

★ ★ ★ ★ ★

FROM SHELL SHOCK TO SPOILED

If there ever was a pampered pup, Rin Tin Tin was it. He dined on choice cut steak to the soothing tunes of classical music. He died in the arms of actress Jean Harlow (or so legend says). His remains are buried in a Paris suburb in a renowned pet cemetery called Cimetiere des Chiens.

A sharp German shepherd with a knack for barking on cue, the original Rin Tin Tin was found with his tail between his legs in a bombed-out animal shelter in France near the end of World War I. Not long after the dog's rescue, American

WHAT'S WITH THE NAME?
Rin Tin Tin was named after a puppet called Rintintin, which a French child gave to American soldier Lee Duncan during World War I for good luck.

serviceman Lee Duncan flew him home to Los Angeles, taught him a few tricks (he had a thirteen-foot long jump), and nicknamed him "Rinty." While leaping for a Frisbee at a California dog show, Rinty caught the eye of producer Darryl F. Zanuck, who recruited him to take the place of the stubborn wolf he had been trying to film in *The Man from Hell's River* (1922). His popularity took off as he became one of the first animals to launch a highly successful movie career. He filmed *Where the North Begins* (1923), *Shadows of the North* (1923), and an array of other doggie rescue flicks. After "hosting" a short-lived 1930 radio program called *The Wonder Dog* (he did his own barking), brave Rin Tin Tin earned his right to Hollywood stardom and became the hero of ABC's *The Adventures of Rin Tin Tin*—but what most people do not know is that the original star of the show was only one of three dogs in front of the camera. In fact, the other German shepherds (Rin Tin Tin II and Rin Tin Tin Jr.) were of no blood relation to the original at all.

★ ★ ★ ★ ★

COME HERE, GIRL! I MEAN ... BOY!

Known around the world for playing friend to a curious little boy named Timmy, **Lassie was played by a young collie named Pal** and a number of his (yes, his) offspring by the same name. Although Timmy referred to his animal pal as a girl, most dogs who played the role were male because their coats were fuller and shinier. Male dogs were also stronger and able to complete the difficult stunts on set.

THREE THINGS YOU NEVER KNEW ABOUT... MR. ED

- The horse's real name was Bamboo Harvester, but a second horse was often used as a stand-in for publicity work.
- In the 1990s, a rumor circulated that Mr. Ed had been a zebra painted solid white, which viewers never figured out because of black and white television. The story was a hoax.
- The horse is buried near Tahlequah, Oklahoma.

★ ★ ★ ★ ★

THEY CALL HIM FLIPPER...

The role of Flipper, the famous bottlenose dolphin, was actually filled by several different dolphins. The first was Mitzi, a female who was the first pupil of famed dolphin trainer Milton Santini. Mitzi did all her stunts except for the famous tail walking, which was done by a male dolphin named Mr. Gipper. Mitzi died of a heart attack when she was fourteen, and is buried at the Dolphin Research Center. Her grace is the first stop on a tour for visitors, where they read a simple plaque in Mitzi's honor. It reads:

Dedicated to the Memory of Mitzi

The original Flipper

1958 – 1972

The last dolphin to serve in the famous role was Bebe, who specialized in high-jumping tricks, and was the longest survivor following the series. She was born at the Seaquarium, where she lived for forty years, giving birth to a calf just months before her death.

Chapter 6

★

Hollywood Aliases from A to Z

Hollywood Aliases from A to Z

★ ★ ★ ★ ★ ★ ★ ★ ★ ★ ★ ★ ★ ★ ★ ★

Rip Torn is without a doubt a cooler name than "Elmore Rual Torn," and Michael Caine flows off the tongue much more smoothly than "Maurice Joseph Micklewhite." Hollywood has been fooling you for years with romantic, ear-catching names that make aspiring actors and actresses sound like superstars before you even see them on screen, but many of them are hiding from the wacky names their parents dared to dub them.

The Estevez family is well known in Hollywood. Father Ramon (Martin Sheen) created his stage name using Rev. Fulton J. Sheen's last name. He and his son Charlie are very close, often playing father-son roles, leading Charlie to use the Sheen name himself. Oldest son Ramon has been known to use both Sheen and Estevez, while the other Estevez children, Emilio and Renée, chose to keep the family name.

109

★ ★ ★ ★ ★

"A"

Alias: Alan Alda, played Hawkeye in *M*A*S*H*
Actual Name: Alphonso Joseph D'Abruzzo

Alias: Jason Alexander, played George on *Seinfeld*
Actual Name: Jason Scott Greenspan

Alias: Tim Allen, played Tim on *Home Improvement*
Actual Name: Tim Allen Dick

Alias: Woody Allen, writer and director
Actual Name: Allen Stewart Konigsberg

Alias: Kirstie Alley, played Rebecca Howe on *Cheers*
Actual Name: Gladys Leeman

Alias: Julie Andrews, starred in *The Sound of Music*
Actual Name: Julia Elizabeth Wells

Alias: Jennifer Aniston, played Rachel on *Friends*
Actual Name: Jennifer Linn Anastassakis

Alias: Desi Arnaz, co-star of *I Love Lucy*
Actual Name: Desiderio Alberto Arnaz y de Acha III

Alias: Rosanna Arquette, starred in *Desperately Seeking Susan* and *Pulp Fiction*
Actual Name: Rosanna Lauren

Alias: Bea Arthur, played Maude on *The Golden Girls*
Actual Name: Bernice Frankel

Alias: Fred Astaire, actor and dancer
Actual Name: Frederick Austerlitz

★ ★ ★ ★ ★

"B"

Alias: Lauren Bacall, played Hannah in *The Mirror Has Two Faces*
Actual Name: Betty Joan Perske

Alias: Catherine Bach, played Daisy Duke in *The Dukes of Hazzard*
Actual Name: Catherine Bachman

Alias: Lucille Ball, star of *I Love Lucy*
Actual Name: Diane Belmont

Alias: Anne Bancroft, played Mrs. Robinson in *The Graduate*
Actual Name: Anna Maria Luisa Italiano

Alias: Warren Beatty, played in *Bonnie and Clyde* and *Dick Tracy*
Actual Name: Henry Warren Beatty

Alias: Bonnie Bedelia, played Holly McClane in *Die Hard*
Actual Name: Bonnie Culkin

> ### IT'S ALL RELATIVE
> Warren Beatty's sister is Shirley MacLaine. He is also the godfather of Melanie Griffith's son Alexander and uncle of Sachi Parker.

Alias: Tom Berenger, played Butch Cassidy in *Butch and Sundance: The Early Days*
Actual Name: Thomas Michael Moore

Alias: Milton Berle, comedian
Actual Name: Milton Berlinger

Alias: Ernest Borgnine, played Ted Denslow in *BASEketball*
Actual Name: Ermes Effron Borgino

Alias: Charles Bronson, played Danny Velinski in *The Great Escape*
Actual Name: Charles Buchinsky

Alias: Mel Brooks, directed *Blazing Saddles*
Actual Name: Melvin Kaminsky

Mel Brooks is one of the few people to have won an Oscar, an Emmy, a Grammy, and a Tony. In fact, he has 3 Emmys, 3 Tonys, and 3 Grammys. Now if he could just get two more Oscars, he'd be set.

Alias: George Burns, played in *Oh God!*
Actual Name: Nathanial Birnbaum

Alias: Richard Burton, played in *Who's Afraid of Virginia Woolf?*
Actual Name: Richard Walter Jenkins Jr.

★ ★ ★ ★ ★

"C"

Alias: Nicolas Cage, played Castor Troy in *Face Off*
Actual Name: Nicolas Coppola

Alias: Michael Caine, played Alfred in *Batman Begins*
Actual Name: Maurice Joseph Micklewhite

DID YOU KNOW

Michael Caine was formally knighted in November 2000 for his contributions to the performing arts. Although knighted under his real name, he is known professionally as Sir Michael Caine.

Alias: Kate Capshaw, played Willie in *Indiana Jones and the Temple of Doom*
Actual Name: Kathleen Sue Nail

Alias: Captain Kangaroo
Actual Name: Robert Keeshan

Alias: Tia Carrere, played Cassandra Wong in *Wayne's World*
Actual Name: Althea Janairo

Alias: Phoebe Cates, played Linda in *Fast Times at Ridgemont High*
Actual Name: Phoebe Katz

Alias: Kim Cattrall, played Samantha Jones on *Sex and the City*
Actual Name: Clare Woodgate

Kim Cattrall once said that she realized fans didn't like the ending of *Sex and the City* because they figured her character, Samantha Jones, would have left her younger boyfriend within a few weeks.

Alias: Cedric the Entertainer, played in *Barbershop*
Actual Name: Cedric Kyles

Alias: Jackie Chan, famous for martial arts movies
Actual Name: Chan Kong-Sang

Alias: Chevy Chase, played Ty Webb in *Caddyshack*
Actual Name: Cornelius Crane Chase

Alias: Gary Cooper, starred in *High Noon* and *Sergeant York*
Actual Name: Frank James Cooper

Alias: David Copperfield
Actual Name: David Kotkin

Alias: Joan Crawford, starred in *What Ever Happened to Baby Jane?*
Actual Name: Lucille Le Sueur

Alias: Bing Crosby, actor and singer
Actual Name: Harry Lillis Crosby

Alias: Tom Cruise, played Joel in *Risky Business*
Actual Name: Thomas Cruise Mapother IV

Tom Cruise was the first actor to star in the films that won the Academy Award for Best Picture (*Rain Man*) and the Razzie for Worst Picture (*Cocktail*) in the same year.

★ ★ ★ ★ ★

"D"

Alias: Ted Danson, played Sam Malone on *Cheers*
Actual Name: Edward Bridge Danson III

Alias: Tony Danza, played Anthony on *Who's The Boss*
Actual Name: Anthonio Ladanza

Alias: James Dean, starred in *Rebel Without a Cause*
Actual Name: James Byron

Alias: Rebecca DeMornay, played Lana in *Risky Business*
Actual Name: Rebecca George

Alias: Catherine Deneuve, French actress
Actual Name: Catherine Dorleac

Alias: Bo Derek, starred in *10*
Actual Name: Mary Cathleen Collins

Alias: Susan Dey, played Laurie Partridge on *The Partridge Family*
Actual Name: Susan Smith

Alias: Angie Dickinson, star of TV series *Police Woman*
Actual Name: Angeline Brown

Alias: Vin Diesel, played Dominic in *The Fast and the Furious*
Actual Name: Mark Vincent

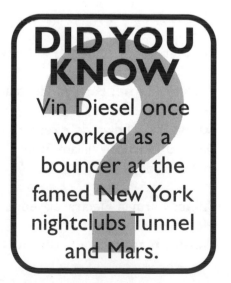

DID YOU KNOW

Vin Diesel once worked as a bouncer at the famed New York nightclubs Tunnel and Mars.

115

CHEESY MOMENTS WITH KIRK DOUGLAS

Kirk Douglas celebrated his bar mitzvah twice—once at age 13 and later at age 83.

He wore lifts in many of his movies, making him appear 5'11" or 6' instead of his actual height—5'9".

Alias: Phyllis Diller, comedian and actress
Actual Name: Phyllis Driver

Alias: Kirk Douglas, played Ned Land in *20,000 Leagues Under The Sea*
Actual Name: Issur Danielovitch Demsky

★ ★ ★ ★ ★

"E"

Alias: Barbara Eden, played the genie on *I Dream of Jeannie*
Actual Name: Barbara Huffman

Alias: Blake Edwards, director
Actual Name: William Blake McEdwards

Alias: Carmen Electra, played Lani McKenzie on *Baywatch*
Actual Name: Tara Leigh Patrick

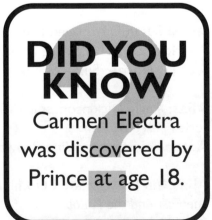

DID YOU KNOW
Carmen Electra was discovered by Prince at age 18.

Alias: Elvira, a.k.a. Mistress of the Dark
Actual Name: Cassandra Peterson

Alias: Linda Evans, played Krystle Grant Jennings Carrington on *Dynasty*
Actual Name: Linda Evanstad

★ ★ ★ ★ ★

"F"

Alias: Jamie Farr, played Klinger in M*A*S*H*
Actual Name: Jameel Joseph Farah

Alias: Douglas Fairbanks, played the Earl of Huntingdon in *Robin Hood*
Actual Name: Douglas Elton Ulman

Alias: Morgan Fairchild, played in *Falcon Crest*
Actual Name: Patsy Ann McClenny

Alias: Sally Field, played Mrs. Gump in *Forrest Gump*
Actual Name: Sally Mahoney

Alias: Glenn Ford, played in *Blackboard Jungle* and *Cimarron*
Actual Name: Gwyilyn Ford

Alias: Jodie Foster, played Clarice Sterling in *Silence of the Lambs*
Actual Name: Alicia Christian Foster

Alias: Michael J. Fox, played in *Family Ties*, *Back to the Future*, and *Spin City*
Actual Name: Michael Andrew Fox

Michael J. Fox was chosen to play Alex P. Keaton on *Family Ties* only after Matthew Broderick turned down the role.

Alias: Jamie Foxx, played Max in *Collateral*
Actual Name: Eric Bishop

Alias: Redd Foxx, played Fred G. Sanford (named after his brother) in *Sanford and Son*
Actual Name: John Elroy Sanford

★ ★ ★ ★ ★

"G"

Alias: Zsa Zsa Gabor, played Jane Avril in *Moulin Rouge* (1952)
Actual Name: Sari Gabor

Alias: Greta Garbo, actress
Actual Name: Greta Lovisa Gustafsson

Alias: Andy Garcia, played Vincent in *The Godfather III*
Actual Name: Andres Arturo Garci-Menendez

Alias: Judy Garland, played Dorothy in *The Wizard of Oz*
Actual Name: Frances Ethel Gumm

Alias: James Garner, played Marshal Zane Cooper in *Maverick*
Actual Name: James Scott Baumgarner

Alias: Mel Gibson, played Rev. Graham Hess in *Signs*
Actual Name: Mel Columcille Gerard Gibson

DID YOU KNOW
Mel Gibson's name means "honey" in Portuguese.

Alias: Whoopi Goldberg, played Oda Mae Brown in *Ghost*
Actual Name: Caryn Johnson

Alias: Elliott Gould, played Ross and Monica's dad on *Friends*
Actual Name: Elliott Goldstein

Alias: Cary Grant, actor
Actual Name: Archibald Leach

Alias: Peter Graves, played Captain Clarence Oveur in *Airplane!*
Actual Name: Peter Aurness

Alias: Joel Grey, played in *Cabaret*
Actual Name: Joel Katz

Alias: Robert Guillaume, played in *Benson* and TV series *Soap*
Actual Name: Robert Peter Williams

★ ★ ★ ★ ★

"H"

Alias: Arsenio Hall, played Winston in *The Real Ghostbusters*
Actual Name: Chuckton Arthur Hall

Alias: Rex Harrison, played in *My Fair Lady*
Actual Name: Reginald Carey

Alias: Mary Hart, host of *Entertainment Tonight*
Actual Name: Mary Johanna Harum

Alias: Rita Hayworth, played Gilda in *Gilda*
Actual Name: Margarita Carmen Cansino

Alias: Pee Wee Herman of *Pee Wee's Play House*
Actual Name: Paul Rubenfeld, aka Paul Reubens

Alias: Charlton Heston, played Henry Hooker in *Tombstone*
Actual Name: John Charles Carter

Alias: Hulk Hogan, television wrestler
Actual Name: Terry Bollea

Alias: William Holden, played in *The Wild Bunch*
Actual Name: William Beedle

Alias: Bob Hope, comedian
Actual Name: Leslie Townes Hope

Alias: Harry Houdini, magician, escape artist
Actual Name: Erich Weiss

Alias: Rock Hudson, actor
Actual Name: Roy Scherer Jr.

★ ★ ★ ★ ★

"J"

Alias: Angelina Jolie, played Lara Croft in *Tomb Raider*
Actual Name: Angelina Jolie Voight

Angelina Jolie has appeared in music videos for Meatloaf, Lenny Kravitz, Antonello Venditti, and The Lemonheads.

Alias: Grace Jones, played May in *A View To Kill*
Actual Name: Grace Mendoza

Alias: James Earl Jones, voice of Darth Vader in *Star Wars*
Actual Name: Todd Jones

Alias: Spike Jonze, director
Actual Name: Adam Spiegel

★ ★ ★ ★ ★

"K"

Alias: Madeline Kahn, played Lili Von Shtupp in *Blazing Saddles*
Actual Name: Madeline Gail Wolfson

Alias: Casey Kasem, Shaggy's voice on *Scooby-Doo* cartoons
Actual Name: Kemal Amin Kasem

Alias: Diane Keaton, played Annie in *Annie Hall*
Actual Name: Diane Hall

Alias: Michael Keaton, played Batman in *Batman*
Actual Name: Michael Douglas

Alias: Larry King, TV personality
Actual Name: Larry Zieger

Alias: Ben Kingsley, played Itzhak Stern in *Schindler's List*
Actual Name: Krishna Banji

★ ★ ★ ★ ★

"L"

Alias: Michael Landon, played Pa on *Little House on the Prairie*
Actual Name: Eugene Maurice Orowitz

Alias: Nathan Lane, played Albert Goldman in *The Bird Cage*
Actual Name: Joseph Lane

Alias: Larry from *The Three Stooges*
Actual Name: Louis Fienberg

> Nathan Lane chose his stage name after the character Nathan Detroit from the musical *Guys and Dolls*.

Alias: Piper Laurie, played Sarah Packard in *The Hustler*
Actual Name: Rosetta Jacobs

Alias: Bruce Lee, actor in martial arts movies.
Actual Name: Lee Yuan Kam (also spelled Lee Jun Fan)

Alias: Vivien Leigh, played Scarlett in *Gone With The Wind*
Actual Name: Vivien Mary Hartley

Alias: Bela Lugosi, played Count Dracula in *Dracula*
Actual Name: Be'la Ferenc Dezso Blasko

★ ★ ★ ★ ★

"M"

Alias: Elle MacPherson, played Blanche Ingram in *Jane Eyre*
Actual Name: Eleanor Gow

Alias: Jayne Mansfield, played Jerri Jordan in *The Girl Can't Help It*
Actual Name: Vera Jane Palmer

Alias: Dean Martin, played Matt Helm in *Murderers' Row*
Actual Name: Dino Crocetti

Alias: Harpo Marx, comedian
Actual Name: Adolph Marx

Alias: Walter Matthau, played in *The Odd Couple*
Actual Name: Walter Matuschanskayasky

Alias: Groucho Marx
Actual Name: Julius Henry Marx

Alias: Marilyn Monroe, played Sugar Kane in *Some Like It Hot*
Actual Name: Norma Jeane Mortenson

Alias: Demi Moore, played Erin Grant in *Striptease*
Actual Name: Demetria Gene Guynes

★ ★ ★ ★ ★

"P"

Alias: Lou Diamond Phillips, played Jose Chavez y Chavez in *Young Guns*
Actual Name: Lou Upchurch

Alias: Natalie Portman, played Padme in *Star Wars*
Actual Name: Natalie Hershlag

Alias: Roman Polanski, director
Actual Name: Raimund Liebling

Roman Polanski fled to Europe after he was accused of raping a thirteen-year-old girl.

Alias: Stefanie Powers, played in TV series *Hart to Hart*
Actual Name: Stafdnia Zofija Federkiewicz

★ ★ ★ ★ ★

"R"

Alias: Tony Randall, played Felix Unger on *The Odd Couple*
Actual Name: Leonard Rosenberg

Alias: Della Reese, played Tess on *Touched by an Angel*
Actual Name: Delloreese Patricia Early

Alias: Debbie Reynolds, played in *Singin' in the Rain*
Actual Name: Mary Frances Reynolds

Alias: Joan Rivers, TV personality
Actual Name: Joan Alexandra Molinsky

Alias: The Rock, played Mathayus in *The Scorpion King*
Actual Name: Dwayne Douglas Johnson

Alias: Ginger Rogers, actress and dancer
Actual Name: Virginia Katherine McMath

Alias: Mickey Rooney, played Mr. Yunioshi in *Breakfast at Tiffany's*
Actual Name: Mickey McGuire

Alias: Meg Ryan, played Sally Albright in *When Harry Met Sally*
Actual Name: Margaret Mary Emily Anne Hyra

WORK AND LOVE DON'T MIX

Shortly after Meg Ryan met Anthony Edwards on the set of *Top Gun*, the two actors began dating and moved in together. A short while later, she met Dennis Quaid while filming *Innerspace*. and dumped Edwards for Quaid, whom she eventually married. Before the two divorced, Ryan was linked romantically to Russell Crowe, whom she met while working on *Proof of Life*.

Alias: Winona Ryder, played Lydia in *Beetlejuice*
Actual Name: Winona Laura Horowitz

★ ★ ★ ★ ★

"S"

Alias: Susan Sarandon, played Louise in *Thelma and Louise*
Actual Name: Susan Abigail Tomalin

Alias: Dick Sargent, played Darrin #2 on *Bewitched*
Actual Name: Richard Cox

Alias: Peter Sellers, played in Pink Panther movies
Actual Name: Richard Henry Sellers

Alias: Jane Seymour, played Dr. Quinn on *Dr. Quinn, Medicine Woman*
Actual Name: Joyce Penelope Wilhelmina Frankenburg

Alias:: Charlie Sheen, played Dep. Mayor Charlie Crawford on *Spin City*
Actual Name: Carlos Irwin Estevez

Alias: Martin Sheen, played President Bartlet on *West Wing*
Actual Name: Ramon Estevez

Alias: Christian Slater, played Daniel in *The Good Shepherd*
Actual Name: Christian Michael Leonard Hawkins

Alias: Anna Nicole Smith, actress
Actual Name: Vickie Lynn Hogan

Anna Nicole Smith met her oil-tycoon husband while she was working as a topless dancer in Houston.

Alias: Kevin Spacey, played Detective Wallace in *Edison*
Actual Name: Kevin Spacey Fowler

Alias: Sylvester Stallone, starred in *Rocky* and *Rambo* movies
Actual Name: Michael Sylvester Enzio Stallone

Alias: Meryl Streep, played in *Sophie's Choice* and *Bridges of Madison County*
Actual Name: Mary Louise Streep

★ ★ ★ ★ ★

"T"

Alias: Mr. T, played Clubber Lang in *Rocky III*
Actual Name: Lawrence Tureaud

Alias: Robert Taylor, played Armand in *Camille*
Actual Name: Spangler Arlington Brugh

Alias: Jonathan Taylor Thomas, played Randy on *Home Improvement*
Actual Name: Jonathan Taylor Weiss

Alias: Rip Torn, played Agent Zed in *Men in Black*
Actual Name: Elmore Rual Torn Jr.

Alias: Lana Turner, played in *Peyton Place*
Actual Name: Julia Jean Mildred Frances Turner

★ ★ ★ ★ ★

"V"

Alias: Jean Claude van Damme, played Jacques Kristoff in *Derailed*
Actual Name: Jean-Claude Camille Francois van Varenberg

Jean-Claude van Damme says he learned English from watching *The Flintstones*.

★ ★ ★ ★ ★

"W"

Alias: Lindsay Wagner, played Jaime on *The Bionic Woman*
Actual Name: Lindsay Jean Ball

Alias: Christopher Walken, played Frank Abagnale Sr. in *Catch Me If You Can*
Actual Name: Ronald Walken

Alias: Burt Ward, played Robin in *Batman* (1960s series)
Actual Name: Bert John Gervis Jr.

Alias: John Wayne
Actual Name: Marion Michael Morrison

Alias: Sigourney Weaver, played Ellen Ripley in *Alien*
Actual Name: Susan Weaver

Alias: Adam West, played Batman in *Batman* (1960s series)
Actual Name: William West Anderson

128

Alias: Vanna White from *Wheel of Fortune*
Actual Name: Vanna Marie Rosich

Alias: Gene Wilder, played The Waco Kid in *Blazing Saddles*
Actual Name: Jerome Silberman

Chapter 7

✰

Where Are They Now? The Skinny on Child Stars

Where Are They Now?
The Skinny on Child Stars

★ ★ ★ ★ ★ ★ ★ ★ ★ ★ ★ ★ ★ ★ ★ ★ ★

From getting busted for drug possession and dodging rumors of their deaths, to fighting for animal rights and sharing their faith, here's the scoop on what your favorite child stars have been doing since the spotlights faded.

DID YOU KNOW?

Malcom-Jamal Warner was named after Malcolm X and jazz pianist Ahmed Jamal. Warner won *Celebrity Poker Showdown* in 2003 in record time. The regular two-hour show only had enough material to fill one hour.

★ ★ ★ ★ ★

THE BUSTED BUD: BILLY GRAY

Nominated for an Emmy Award at just twenty-one years old for his portrayal of Bud Anderson on the 1950s sitcom *Father Knows Best*, **Billy Gray became known as one of the first child stars to be busted for possession of drugs** when his stash of marijuana earned him more than a month behind bars in 1962. Since then, he has insisted that the arrest ruined his career, and he has been dodging accusations of addiction ever since. In 1998, Gray settled a libel suit with popular movie critic Leonard Maltin, who mistakenly called him a drug addict while reviewing the 1974 movie *Dusty and Sweets McGee* in one of his film guides. Today, Gray is an inventor—he created the F-1 Guitar Pick—and an avid Speedway motorcycle racer. His bike, the Orange Blossom Special, was named by a clever announcer at California's Irwindale Speedway in honor of its shiny orange rims.

★ ★ ★ ★ ★

THE BABY BRADY: SUSAN OLSEN

She may have missed the filming of the popular Brady 1988 reunion show, *A Very Brady Christmas,*

because she was busy living it up on her Jamaican honeymoon, but Susan Olsen's years of training at the American Academy of Dramatic Arts was time well spent. Although she has dodged rumors of tarnishing her innocent image in pornographic films (she did not) since her role as Cindy Brady on *The Brady Bunch*, Olsen has worked as a graphic designer, a radio talk-show host, and a spokesperson for Migraine Awareness Month. Her final attempt to shed the annoying reputation that she is still the perky baby Brady—she had surgery to correct that pesky lisp.

★ ★ ★ ★ ★

THE ALIEN'S BEST FRIEND: HENRY THOMAS

In the early 1980s, a shy nine-year-old Thomas walked onto the set of the blockbuster hit *ET: Extra Terrestrial* with almost no experience to try out for the part of the loveable, curious Elliott. Regardless of his green ways, director Steven Spielberg gave him a shot and cast him in the part of a lifetime. After the media attention for his performance died down, however, Thomas did a few more small films and at just thirteen years old left Hollywood for a sales job behind the counter at a video store. He took some time to recover from his short-lived fame while studying at Blinn College in College Station, Texas.

Although a little embarrassed of his namesake, Thomas wouldn't be gone from show biz for long. In 1994, he left his childhood reputation behind and reappeared on screen as Brad Pitt's brother Samuel in *Legends of the Fall* and the sinister Johnny Sirocco in *Gangs of New York*.

★ ★ ★ ★ ★

THE HOTHEAD HUXTABLE: MALCOLM-JAMAL WARNER

After starring as the charming big brother Theo Huxtable on *The Cosby Show*, Malcolm-Jamal Warner moved on from acting and stepped behind the camera to produce shows like *Malcolm & Eddie* and *Fresh Prince of Bel Air*. Today, he rocks out on the electric guitar and upright bass in his popular jazz band, Miles Long. He says fans are surprised to see him in dreadlocks behind the microphone, and if they slip up and call him Theo, he is quick to correct them with his real name.

★ ★ ★ ★ ★

THE STRAIGHT-LACED SIBLINGS: CANDACE AND KIRK CAMERON

Known as a straight-A student and the best friend to nosy neighbor Kimmie Gibbler, actress Candace Cameron played big sister D.J. Tanner on the family-friendly ABC series *Full House* from 1987-1995. The real-life sister of *Growing Pains* star Kirk Cameron, she spent her teenage years mingling among other Hollywood youngsters. While filming the eight-year series, she studied at California's Chatsworth High School with fellow young actresses Lori Beth Denberg (of Nickelodeon's *All That*) and Lindsay Sloane (of USA's *Sabrina the Teenage Witch*). After *Full House* came to a close and Cameron taped a stint of cheesy Lifetime movies, she married pro hockey player Valeri Bure and today stays at home with her three children, Natasha, Lev, and Maksim.

As for Kirk, he has taken his religious ways to the street as the cofounder of Living Water Ministries and The Way of the Master Ministries, which chronicles street evangelism in a Christian television series. He also started Camp Firefly, a refuge for children suffering from terminal illnesses. When he's not witnessing for Jesus, Cameron is playing parent to six children with wife and fellow *Growing Pains* star Chelsea Noble, whom he married in 1991.

Both Candace and Kirk have announced that because of their commitment to the Christian faith, they will no longer accept roles that compromise their values (that means no nude scenes).

★ ★ ★ ★ ★

THE MORAL MAKER: JERRY MATHERS

Known as Theodore "Beaver" Cleaver in the wholesome 1950s and '60s classic *Leave It to Beaver*, Jerry Mathers is known as one of the first childhood actors to ever receive a percentage of a sitcom's merchandise revenue. To this day, he makes money off his boyhood gig, which first went on air October 4, 1957. After the show's producers called it quits after seven years, Mathers finished high school and got a degree in philosophy from the University of California, Berkeley. Before giving in to the daily grind of adulthood as a banker and real estate developer, he tried his hand at fame and fortune one last time in a band named Beaver and The Trappers. After a few summers of cutting records, he entered the real world and today is a motivational speaker, traveling the country shaming the moral decline of America with all the lessons *Leave It to Beaver* has to offer.

> ## THREE THINGS YOU NEVER KNEW ABOUT... JERRY MATHERS
>
> - The Associated Press released reports that he had died while serving in the Air Force National Guard during the Vietnam War, but it was a mix-up with a soldier who had a similar name.
> - He sells autographed photos of himself for $50 online.
> - He was once a spokesman for the National Psoriasis Foundation.

★ ★ ★ ★ ★

THE SPOILED RICH GIRL: LISA WHELCHEL

Blair Warner from *The Facts of Life* was known to worship herself every now and then, but offscreen actress Lisa Whelchel was a humbled-hearted Christian. In fact, her faith caused trouble with the cast when scriptwriters wrote an episode about Blair having sex with her crush. Strongly believing in the need for teens to wait until marriage before jumping between the sheets, Whelchel refused to do the part. Today, she is a mother and the author of several books on homeschooling and parenting. She recently came under fire for her "hot sauce on the tongue" suggestion in one of her books, which recommends parents discipline their children with a little drop of the burning condiment.

★ ★ ★ ★ ★

THE TWO COREYS: COREY FELDMAN AND COREY HAIM

Famous for their onscreen duos in the 1980s, Feldman and Haim first made their mark on the film industry when they played Edgar Frog and Sam Emerson in cult classic vampire flick *The Lost Boys.* Afterwards, they became so popular as best pals that they made seven more movies together. However, as they got older, the two heartthrobs got burnt out on being on the set so often. They had a falling out, took a break to regain their individual identities, and never looked back. The son of famous songwriter/producer Bob Feldman, who wrote 1950s hits like "My Boyfriend's Back," today Feldman is spicing up his career with an array of cheesy appearances on reality television shows like VH1's *The Surreal Life,* and is working on a music career with his first solo album, *Former Child Actor.* Haim recently kicked a long-time drug addiction that caused him to have a minor stroke in 2001, and now works in a Toronto record store while still pursuing a career in acting.

★ ★ ★ ★ ★

THE VOICE OF SIMBA: JONATHAN TAYLOR THOMAS

Known as the voice of young Simba on the popular Disney flick *The Lion King,* and as the heartthrob middle child, Randy, on *Home Improvement,* JTT lured a whole new audience to the ABC tool-man show in the 1990s—an audience interested in anything but hot rods and Binford saws. After seven seasons, Thomas quit the show to go to college—it was a toss-up between a handful of Ivy League academies. He picked Harvard (and spent some time at the University of Saint Andrews in Scotland) and today is known for speaking out against abortion, and for doing a lot of cartoon voiceover work.

★ ★ ★ ★ ★

THE POSSESSED PRETTY GIRL: LINDA BLAIR

She may have been nominated for the 1973 Best Supporting Actress Academy Award at the ripe age of fifteen for her work spitting pea soup in the legendary horror flick *The Exorcist*, but today Linda Blair spends her time praising pleather and defending the rights of animals with PETA. She owns her own clothing line (Linda Blair's Wild West Collection) and is the author of a book about her animal-friendly eating habits called *Going Vegan!*

THREE THINGS YOU NEVER KNEW ABOUT... LINDA BLAIR

- In 1985, she was mocked with a Razzie Award for Worst Career Achievement as the queen of scream.

- After *The Exorcist* premiered in 1973, she had to hire policemen to stay at her family home because of all the death threats she received from frightened fans.

- To the surprise of many Hollywood veterans, Blair did not have a body double in the 1979 disco flick *Roller Boogie*. She did all of her own skating.

★ ★ ★ ★ ★

The Munster Man: Butch Patrick

Since sporting a widow's peak and playing with his famous woof-woof doll on *The Munsters* in 1964, child actor Butch Patrick has made friends with the rival family—he dated actress Lisa Loring, who played Wednesday Addams on *The Addams Family*. In the 1980s, Patrick formed the one-hit wonder band Eddie and the Monsters, best associated with the little known single "Whatever Happened to Eddie?" Although they were featured on *Basement Tapes*, a short-lived MTV show for unsigned bands, they never made it big as musicians. Today, Patrick spends every October dressing up as Eddie Munster for Halloween parties and sells woof-woof replicas on www.Munsters.com.

★ ★ ★ ★ ★

The Starlet Turned Recluse: Deanna Durbin

The Shirley Temple of the 1930s who grew famous alongside fellow singing actress Judy Garland, Deanna Durbin was the highest paid actress of her time. She won a juvenile Oscar for her work in the 1936 flick *Three Smart Girls* the same year Garland won for *The Wizard of Oz*, but in 1948, at 27 years old, she left Hollywood for a little peace and quiet. Today, she is a widow and protects her right to privacy in Paris, where she continues to refuse all requests for interviews.

THREE THINGS YOU NEVER KNEW ABOUT... DEANNA DURBIN

- She was considered to play Dorothy in *The Wizard of Oz* (1939).

- In 1980, she sent a photo of herself to *Life* magazine to squash rumors among her fans that she had gained weight.

- She was a favorite actress of Winston Churchill and Holocaust victim Anne Frank. Frank allegedly kept photos of Durbin in her secret Amsterdam annex, and Churchill used to request private screenings of her films before they were released in Great Britain.

★ ★ ★ ★ ★

ONE OF THE GANG: ROBERT BLAKE

Although he is more recently known for his acquittal of murder charges, child star Robert Blake (or Mickey Gubitosi, as he was known as a boy) got his start at just five years old in the series *Our Gang*. One of the more popular members of the rowdy gang, his career continued to blossom when he won parts in a number of films, including the coveted role of Little Beaver in the

Red Ryder Western series. Today, he still hasn't lost his passion for cowboy ways, and after he was let off the hook for the murder of his wife in 2005, he told several journalists that he was going to get a van and head out west. However innocent he may be, Blake has inspired many fellow actors in the art of playing the bad guy. His performances in *Baretta* and *In Cold Blood* were a help to Anthony Hopkins as he prepared for his creepy role as Hannibal Lecter.

★ ★ ★ ★ ★

THE ORIGINAL MOUSEKETEER: ANNETTE FUNICELLO

The Mickey Mouse Club has served as a launching pad for countless child stars, and Annette Funicello is no exception. Her roles sporting a one-piece in the sand led her to an adulthood full of beach flicks with Italian-American teen idol Frankie Avalon and chart-topping pop singles like "Tall Paul" and "Pineapple Princess." Unfortunately, while filming *Back to the*

THREE THINGS YOU NEVER KNEW ABOUT ANNETTE FUNICELLO

- When Walt Disney cast her in her first beach movie, he asked her to avoid the temptation to show off her slim body in a bikini because a one-piece swimsuit would better uphold her wholesome image.

- Her son, Jason Gilardi, is in the rock band Caroline's Spine and played himself in her biographical movie, *A Dream Is a Wish Your Heart Makes*.

- Singer/songwriter Paul Anka wrote his hit single "Puppy Love" about how he had a crush on her.

Beach in 1987, Funicello was diagnosed with multiple sclerosis and has since set up the Annette Funicello Fund for Neurological Disorders. She announced her battle with the disorder in 1992, and in 1995, told her story in the biographical made-for-TV-movie, *A Dream Is a Wish Your Heart Makes: The Annette Funicello Story.*

★ ★ ★ ★ ★

THE STINGY PEN PAL: STANLEY LIVINGSTON

Stanley Livingston's portrayal of Chip Douglas may have made him one of the least loved personas on *My Three Sons* in the 1960s (he was known to throw away his fan mail without reading it), but he has since lived down the poor reputation. Livingston continued his youthful fame in a other TV and movie roles, but today he has left the spotlight for good. Instead of pursuing fame for himself, he serves the stars as an artist—his popular stained glass has been purchased by the likes of Tom Hanks and Hugh Hefner.

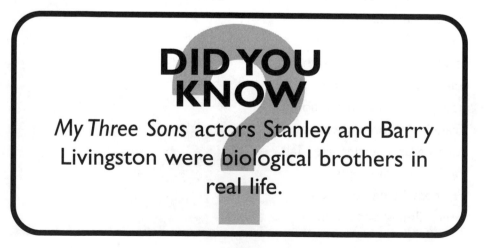

DID YOU KNOW?

My Three Sons actors Stanley and Barry Livingston were biological brothers in real life.

★ ★ ★ ★ ★

THE SHORT-LIVED PARTRIDGE: JEREMY GELBWAKS

Known around the world as Chris Partridge number one on *The Partridge Family*—he was replaced when his father got an out-of-state job transfer in 1971—today, Gelbwaks is a product manager for a computer company in New Orleans. Ironically, New Orleans is also the hometown of drummer Susan Cowsill of The Cowsills, the band upon which *The Partridge Family* story was based.

★ ★ ★ ★ ★

THE STEREOTYPE SMASHER: MARY BADHAM

Famous for her portrayal of the innocent Scout Finch in *To Kill A Mockingbird*, today Badham restores aged art for a living and helps coordinate college testing on the side. She also travels around the world speaking about the importance of tolerance and kindness, messages from her hit childhood movie role. In

THREE THINGS YOU NEVER KNEW ABOUT... MARY BADHAM

- For years after filming *To Kill A Mockingbird*, she kept in touch with actor Gregory Peck and continued to call him Atticus until his death in 2003.

- She is the sister of *Saturday Night Fever* director John Badham.

- In 1963 at just ten years old, she was the youngest ever Academy Award nominee for Best Supporting Actress. She has since lost the record to Tatum O'Neal for the 1973 film *Paper Moon*.

2005, she appeared onscreen for the first time in thirty-eight years in the Cameron Watson film *Our Very Own,* and has since agreed to come out of retirement and consider future roles if the script fits.

★ ★ ★ ★ ★

THE BOLD BRADY: CHRISTOPHER KNIGHT

Since playing curious middle child Peter on *The Brady Bunch*, Christopher Knight has joined a cast of other Hollywood has-beens like Charo on a host of VH1 reality television shows, where he makes a fool of himself for all of America to see. His most recent project, *My Fair Brady*, portrays his relationship with *America's Next Top Model*'s Adrienne Curry, who is half his age. When he's not making jokes about his girlfriend's sexuality on camera, Knight works as a computer nerd (he was once the executive vice president at Eskape Labs) and occasionally makes appearances as his former Peter Brady self in cast reunion flicks like *The Brady Brides* (1981) and *A Very Brady Christmas* (1988).

★ ★ ★ ★ ★

THE BLOSSOMING BRAINIAC: MAYIM BIALIK

Despite rumors that she had died of alcohol poisoning in 1997, the child star who portrayed the brainy babe Blossom Russo in the hit sitcom *Blossom* is alive and well, living the posh life of a smarty-pants

UCLA graduate working toward a Ph.D. in neuroscience. She will still admit, however, that while filming the show during her teenage years, she had a huge crush on TV brother Anthony, played by Michael Stoyanov.

★ ★ ★ ★ ★

AN UPDATE ON OTHER CHILD STARS:

THREE THINGS YOU NEVER KNEW ABOUT... MAYIM BIALIK

According to one of her fan sites, when she was younger, she...

• Loved the band Violent Femmes and the sitcom *Seinfeld.*

• Was named after the Hebrew word for water.

• Pierced her ears nine times in honor of her favorite number (nine).

• **Peter Ostrum**, who played the lead role in *Charlie and the Chocolate Factory*, was offered a contract for three more films by Warner Brothers but declined and quit acting altogether. Today he is a veterinarian in upstate New York.

• **Mindy Cohn**, who played Natalie Green on *The Facts of Life*, graduated from Loyola-Marymount University in 1995 and has since served as the voice of Velma in the cartoon series *What's New Scooby-Doo?* She is also an avid member of weSPARK, a cancer support group.

• **Valerie Bertinelli**, who was known for perfect hair and perky smiles as Barbara Royer on the sitcom *One Day At A Time*, married rocker Eddie Van Halen and joined the cast of a slew of Lifetime movies in the 1980s and 1990s. Things must not have been all smiles, though; the couple divorced in 2005.

- **Ron Howard**, otherwise known as Opie Taylor from *The Andy Griffith Show*, has become a very successful director/producer. He won two Academy Awards and a Directors Guild of America Award for producing and directing *A Beautiful Mind*.

Chapter 8

The Ultimate
Television/Movies Quiz

The Ultimate Television/Movies Quiz

★ ★ ★ ★ ★ ★ ★ ★ ★ ★ ★ ★ ★ ★ ★ ★

So you think you know everything there is to know about the hottest television series and box office movies. Try your hand at the ultimate test of trivia about the best moments 1950-2005 had to offer:

★ ★ ★ ★ ★

WHAT'S IN A NAME: PART 1

1. Mouth and Chunk were the nicknames of what characters in *The Goonies?*

   _____

2. In *Dirty Dancing*, what was Baby's real name?

   _____

3. Bill and Ted introduced several historical figures to Missy in *Bill and Ted's Excellent Adventures.* Who were they?

   _____

4. Name all four Ghostbusters.

   _____

5. In *Labyrinth*, Sarah is trying to save her baby brother. What was his name?

   _____

6. In *Aliens*, what was Newt's real name?

   _____

7. Name the robot from the *Short Circuit* flicks.

   _____

8. In *Ferris Bueller's Day Off,* what is the principal's name? His assistant?

   _____

9. In the 1980s cult classic film *Sixteen Candles*, what was the name of the exchange student kept by Sam's grandparents?

   _____

10. In *Tootsie*, what was the name of the woman played by Dustin Hoffmann?

    _____

★ ★ ★ ★ ★

CAMEO CHARACTERS: TRIVIA ABOUT SPECIAL APPEARANCES

Who was the actor/actress who played...

1. the pretty blond girl Elliot danced with in *ET: The Extra-Terrestrial?*

   _____

2. the burnout at the police station Ferris's sister, Jeanie, kisses in *Ferris Beuller's Day Off?*

   _____

3. Sarah Jessica Parker's best friend in *Girls Just Wanna Have Fun?*

   _____

4. Julie's best friend in *I Still Know What You Did Last Summer?*

   _____

5. Jodie Dallas, the first openly gay character on network television, in the sitcom *Soap?*

   _____

6. Spicolli's sidekicks in *Fast Times at Ridgemont High?*

   _____

7. Karen's divorce lawyer on *Will & Grace?*

   _____

8. the spaceship's voice in *Flight of the Navigator?*

   _____

9. an ambulance driver on the 2005 season of *ER?*

_____

10. an ambulance driver on the 2004 season of *Scrubs?*

_____

OTHER CAMEO TRIVIA

1. What was Judge Smales's grandson's name in *Caddyshack?*

_____

2. What *Cheers* actor appeared in *Star Wars: The Empire Strikes Back?*

_____

3. What famous director makes an appearance at the end of *Blues Brothers?*

_____

4. What famous director often scripted himself into small background roles in his own films?

_____

★ ★ ★ ★ ★

THE DAILY GRIND: TRIVIA ABOUT WORK

1. In *Say Anything*, what did John Cusack say he would never do for a living? What career did he want?

   _____

   _____

2. In *Office Space*, what was Milton's prized possession that Peter pulled from the rubble after Intitech burned to the ground?

   _____

3. What job does Tom Hanks's character have in *Bachelor Party*?

   _____

4. On *The Jeffersons*, what business does George Jefferson own?

   _____

5. On *24*, what agency employs Jack Bauer?

   _____

6. In the movie *Notting Hill,* what magazine does Hugh Grant's character say he works for in an attempt to get an "interview" with the movie star played by Julia Roberts?

   _____

7. What was Adam Sandler's occupation in *Big Daddy*?

   _____

8. In *Midnight Run*, what agency does Walsh (Robert De Niro) work for?

   _____

9. On *Friends*, what were the names of the restaurants where Monica was head chef?

    _____

10. In *Beverly Hills Cop*, Axel Foley enters the hotel and uses an alias. Who does he say he works for, and who is he allegedly going to interview?

    _____

11. What does Michelle say she invented in *Romy and Michelle's High School Reunion*?

    _____

12. Who was the sponsor for *Wayne's World*?

    _____

13. In *The Karate Kid*, what color did Mr. Miagi make Daniel paint his house as part of his training?

    _____

★ ★ ★ ★ ★

Man's Best Friend: Trivia About Animals

1. In *Next Friday*, what name is given to the ferocious dog?

    _____

2. What is the donkey's name in *Shrek*?

    _____

3. In the film *Jumanji*, what is the last animal to stomp through the room after the stampede?

    _____

4. In *Splash,* what does the mermaid choose to name herself after?

   _____

5. What is the name of the animal star whose theme song describes him as "faster than lightning?"

   _____

6. In *The Little Mermaid*, what did the seagull Scuttle name a fork?

   _____

7. By what name is Mickey Mouse known in Italy?

   _____

8. In *Star Trek*, what name does Captain Jean-Luc Picard give his fish?

   _____

9. What kind of a bird kept Robert Blake company on *Baretta?* What was his name?

   _____

★ ★ ★ ★ ★

ON THE ROAD AGAIN: TRIVIA ABOUT TRAVELING

1. In *National Lampoon's Vacation*, what did the legendary Griswald family call their green station wagon?

   _____

2. What kind of car was made famous by *The Dukes of Hazzard?*

   _____

3. In *Spaceballs*, what does the bumper sticker say on the back of Lonestar's ship?

   _____

4. In *Innerspace*, what did Igoe's license plate say?

   _____

5. What was on the license plate of the Ghostbusters' car?

   _____

★ ★ ★ ★ ★

NUMBER CRUNCHERS: TRIVIA ABOUT DIGITS

1. How many days were the castaways on the mysterious island during the first season of *Lost*?

   _____

2. How many gigawatts of electricity did Doc Brown need to power the Delorion in *Back to the Future*?

   _____

3. What was the hottest possible temperature on the Klopek's furnace in *The 'Burbs*?

   _____

4. What was Dirty Harry's badge number?

   _____

5. Above what speed did the bus in the movie *Speed* need to go in order to keep from blowing up?

   _____

6. In *National Lampoon's Animal House,* what is Blutarski's grade-point average?

    _____

7. In *Stripes,* how much money does Ox (John Candy) pay to mud wrestle with women?

    _____

8. In *Monty Python and the Holy Grail,* what number must you count to before throwing the Holy Hand Grenade?

    _____

9. On *The Brady Bunch,* at what address did Mike and Carol Brady live?

    _____

★ ★ ★ ★ ★

WHAT'S IN A NAME: PART II

1. Who ordered the Code Red in *A Few Good Men?*

    _____

2. What big-hearted, underprivileged character did Leonardo DiCaprio play in *Titanic?*

    _____

3. What was the name of Milla Jovovich's character in *The Fifth Element?*

    _____

4. In *Jerry McGuire,* what was the name of Jerry's stepson?

    _____

5. In *Matilda*, what was the name of Matilda's teacher?

    _____

6. In *Fantasia*, what is the name of the Sorcerer?

    _____

7. On *I Love Lucy*, what was Lucy Ricardo's maiden name?

    _____

8. On *Friends*, to what person was Chandler's *TV Guide* delivered?

    _____

★ ★ ★ ★ ★

She Loves Me, She Loves Me Not: Trivia About Relationships

1. Where did Ronald take Cindy for their final date in the movie *Can't Buy Me Love*?

    _____

2. On *Friends*, why did Phoebe and Mike break up?

    _____

3. In *Weird Science*, what don't Gary and Wyatt do when they take a shower with Lisa?

    _____

4. What was the real name of Carrie's lover (Mr. Big) on *Sex and the City*?

5. Which onscreen lover did Gene Kelly make cry by telling her she couldn't dance in *Singin' in the Rain?*

    _____

6. Because the movie *Ghost* was so romantic, what was handed out to women at showings in Mexico?

    _____

★ ★ ★ ★ ★

FAMOUS FIRSTS: TRIVIA ABOUT GROUNDBREAKING HISTORY

Do you know these famous firsts?

1. First feature-length animated film

    _____

2. First (and only) silent film to win an Academy Award

    _____

3. First PG-rated Disney picture

    _____

4. First film with audible dialogue

    _____

5. First black woman to win an Oscar

    _____

6. First person to make $1 million for a single picture

    _____

7. First name Bugs Bunny appeared under in his early 1930s cartoons

    _____

8. First interracial sitcom kiss

    _____

    _____

9. Winner of the first televised Miss America pageant in 1954

    _____

10. First U.S. company to make a commercial featuring lingerie models

    _____

11. First character to speak in the original *Star Wars*

    _____

12. First film in which Pierce Brosnan appeared as James Bond

    _____

13. First woman director to bring in more than $100 million at the box office

    _____

★ ★ ★ ★ ★

GASP! TRIVIA ABOUT SCANDALS

1. Which *Survivor* contestant lied about his grandmother's death to gain sympathy on the show?

   _____

2. Which of President Bartlet's children was kidnapped on *The West Wing?*

   _____

3. What did Livia try to arrange for her son, Tony, on the first season of *The Sopranos?*

   _____

4. What childhood trauma constantly haunted Fox Mulder on *The X Files?*

   _____

5. In *The Breakfast Club*, what was found in Brian's locker that he was going to try to kill himself with?

   _____

6. What was used as blood for the famous shower scene in Alfred Hitchcock's *Psycho?*

   _____

7. On a finale of *Desperate Housewives*, what secret did Mary Alice die to protect?

   _____

8. What was everyone on set of *The Alamo* (2004) told to do to passing news helicopters to keep them from being able to use their footage on television?

_____

Answers

★ ★ ★ ★ ★

WHAT'S IN A NAME: PART 1

1. Clark and Lawrence

2. Frances

3. Socrates, Billy the Kid, Joan of Arc, Sigmund Freud, Genghis Khan, Beethoven, and Abraham Lincoln

4. Peter Venkman, Egon Spengler, Ray Stantz, and Winston Zedmore

5. Toby

6. Rebecca Jorden

7. Johnny

8. Ed Rooney and Grace

9. Long Duk Dong

10. Dorothy Michaels

★ ★ ★ ★ ★

CAMEO CHARACTERS: TRIVIA ABOUT SPECIAL APPEARANCES

Name the actor/actress who played...

1. Erika Eleniak

2. Charlie Sheen

3. Helen Hunt

4. Brandy

5. Billy Crystal

6. Eric Stolz and Anthony Edwards

7. Macaulay Culkin

8. Pee Wee Herman

9. John Stamos

10. Molly Shannon

★ ★ ★ ★ ★

OTHER CAMEO TRIVIA

1. Spaulding

2. John Ratzenberg

3. Steven Spielberg

4. Alfred Hitchcock

★ ★ ★ ★ ★

THE DAILY GRIND: TRIVIA ABOUT WORK

1. He said he would never buy anything, sell anything, or process anything. He wanted to be a kickboxer.

2. The red stapler

3. He is a school bus driver.

4. Dry cleaning

5. CTU

6. *Horse and Hound*

7. Tollbooth worker

8. Mosconi Bail Bonds

9. Alesandro's and Javu

10. *Rolling Stone*, Michael Jackson

11. Post-its

12. Noah's arcade

13. Green

★ ★ ★ ★ ★

Man's Best Friend: Trivia About Animals

1. Chico

2. Donkey

3. A rhinoceros

4. Madison Avenue

5. Flipper

6. Dinglehopper

7. Topolino

8. Livingston

9. Cockatoo, Fred

★ ★ ★ ★ ★

On the Road Again: Trivia About Traveling

1. The Family Truckster

2. 1968 Charger

3. I Love Uranus

4. SNAPON

5. ECTO-1

★ ★ ★ ★ ★

NUMBER CRUNCHERS: TRIVIA ABOUT DIGITS

1. 44

2. 1.21 gigawatts

3. 5,000 degrees

4. 2211

5. 50 mph

6. 0.0

7. $413.58

8. Three... no more, no less

9. 4222 Clinton Way. No city was ever specified.

★ ★ ★ ★ ★

WHAT'S IN A NAME: PART II

1. Colonel Nathan P. Jessup

2. Jack Dawson

3. Lelu

4. Ray

5. Jennifer Honey

6. Yensid (Disney spelled backward)

7.   McGillicuddy

8.   Miss Chanandler Bong

★ ★ ★ ★ ★

SHE LOVES ME, SHE LOVES ME NOT: TRIVIA ABOUT RELATIONSHIPS

1.   An airplane junkyard

2.   He never wanted to get married.

3.   Take off their pants

4.   John

5.   Debbie Reynolds

6.   Envelopes of tissues

★ ★ ★ ★ ★

FAMOUS FIRSTS: TRIVIA ABOUT GROUNDBREAKING HISTORY

1.   *Snow White and the Seven Dwarfs* (1937)

2.   *Wings* (1927)

3.   *The Black Hole* (1979)

4.   *The Jazz Singer* (1927)

5.   Hattie McDaniel

6. Elizabeth Taylor, *Cleopatra*

7. Happy Rabbit

8. *Star Trek* stars Captain James T. Kirk (William Shatner) and Lt. Uhura (Nichelle Nichols) on November 22, 1968

9. Miss California, Lee Ann Meriwether

10. Playtex in 1987

11. C-3PO

12. *Golden Eye* (1995)

13. Penny Marshall for *Big*

★ ★ ★ ★ ★

GASP! TRIVIA ABOUT SCANDALS

1. Jon Dalton

2. Zoey

3. His death.

4. His sister was kidnapped by aliens.

5. A flare gun

6. Chocolate syrup

7. She murdered her son's biological mother.

8. Show them their middle fingers

WHERE WE GOT THIS STUFF

Bathroom Readers' Hysterical Institute. *Uncle John's Bathroom Reader Plunges Into Great Lives*. San Diego: Portable Press, 2003.

Beasley, Jake. *Celebrity Aliases Unmasked*. USA: Sweetwater Press, 2004.

Clarke, John. *The Greatest Rock and Pop Miscellany Ever!* Italy: Sanctuary Publishing, 2004.

Cox, Stephen. *The Beverly Hillbillies*. Nashville: Cumberland House, 2003.

DiFranco, JoAnn and Anthony DiFranco. *Mister Rogers: Good Neighbor to America's Children*. Minneapolis: Dillon Press, 1983.

Epting, Chris. *James Dean Died Here: The Locations of American Pop Culture Landmarks*. Los Angeles: Santa Monica Press, 2003.

Fingeroth, Danny. *Reese Witherspoon*. New York: Rosen Book Works, 2003.

———. *Liv Tyler*. New York: Rosen Book Works, 2003.

———. *Elijah Wood*. New York: Rosen Book Works, 2003.

Grossberg, Josh. "'Bachelor Bob' Sings Lawsuit Blues." December 22, 2003, www.cnn.com.

Hamrick, Craig. "TV Guide's Ultimate Trivia Quiz!" *TV Guide*, August 7, 2005.

Kamm, Jim and Matteo Molinari. *Oops! Movie Mistakes That Made The Cut*. New York: Citadel Press Books, 2002.

Keller, Julie. "Leo Gets a Date... And Lawsuit." November 1, 1999, www.cnn.com.

McCracken, Kristin. *James Van Der Beek*. New York: Rosen Book Works, 2001.

People Magazine, ed. *100 Greatest TV Stars of Our Time*. New York: People Books, 2003.

Petras, Kathryn and Ross. *Unusually Stupid Americans*. New York: Villard Books, 2003.

Roeper, Richard. *Schlock Values: Hollywood at Its Worst*. New York: Hyperion Books, 2004.

Sandys, Jon. *Movie Mistakes*. London: Virgin Books, 2005.

Snipes, Stephanie. "The little dog that could." www.cnn.com, August 20, 2004.

Sova, Dawn B. *Forbidden Films: Censorship Histories of 125 Motion Pictures*. New York: Checkmark Books, 2001.

Stone, Tanya Lee. *Success with an Open Heart: Oprah Winfrey*. Connecticut: The Millbrook Press, 2001.

Stuart, Mel and Josh Young. *Pure Imagination: The Making of Willy Wonka and the Chocolate Factory*. New York: St. Martin's Press, 2002.

Sweetingham, Lisa. "Robert Blake denies plotting to kill his wife." Court TV, October 3, 2005, http://www.courttv.com/trials/blake/100305_ctv.html

Tonks, Douglas. *TV's Most Wanted*. Virginia: Brassey's Inc., 2003.

Vaz, Mark Cotta. *The Lost Chronicles*. New York: Touchstone Television, 2005.
Wheeler, Jill C. *Jessica Simpson*. Minnesota: ABDO Publishing Company, 2005.
Wild, David. *The One With All Ten Years: FRIENDS 'Til the End*. New York: Time, Inc,
    2004.

WE ALSO USED THESE SOURCES:

www.hollywood.com
www.eonline.com
www.imdb.com
www.cagenews.com
www.wikipedia.org
http://lindablairworldheart.com
www.Munsters.com
Former Child Star Central,
http://members.tripod.com/~former_child_star/where.html
www.geocities.com/Hollywood/Academy/5228/ddlgbv.html
www.inthe80s.com
www.inthe90s.com
www.cagefactor.com
http://news.bbc.co.uk/1/hi/entertainment/showbiz/1710311.stm

ABOUT THE AUTHOR

Camille Smith Platt is a freelance writer and the Editor of *Chattanooga Christian Family* magazine. A graduate of the Samford University Department of Journalism and Mass Communication, she has also done research and writing for national trivia magazine *mental_floss* and Birmingham lifestyle magazine *PORTICO*. Her love-hate relationship with trivia stems from a fascination of quirky knowledge and a lifetime of always being stumped. She and her husband, Daniel, live in Chattanooga, Tennessee.

YOU MAY ALSO ENJOY THESE OTHER BOOKS IN THE REAL CHEESY SERIES.

Real Cheesy Facts About: U.S. Presidents

ISBN-13: 978-1-57587-248-3

ISBN-10: 1-57587-248-X

Real Cheesy Facts About: Rock 'n' Roll

ISBN-13: 978-1-57587-251-3

ISBN-10: 1-57587-251-X

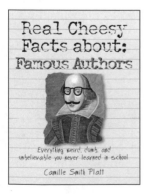

Real Cheesy Facts About: Famous Authors

ISBN-13: 978-1-57587-250-6

ISBN-10: 1-57587-250-1